W9-BNG-762

Chicago Public Library

Form 178 rev. 11-00

Empire of the Islamic World

ROBIN DOAK

Facts On File, Inc.

Great Empires of the Past: EMPIRE OF THE ISLAMIC WORLD

HISTORY CONSULTANT: Dr. Stephen Cory, Ph.D., University of California at Santa Barbara, Department of Religious Studies

Facts On File, Inc.
132 West 31st Street
New York NY 10001

Library of Congress Cataloging-in-Publication Data
Doak, Robin S. (Robin Santos), 1963–
  Empire of the Islamic World / Robin Doak.
    p. cm. – (Great empires of the past)
  Includes bibliographical references and index.
  ISBN 0-8160-5557-2 (hc: alk. paper)
  1. Islamic Empire–Juvenile literature. 2. Civilization,
Islamic–Juvenile literature. I. Title. II. Series.
  DS38.3.D63 2004
  909'.0976701–dc22   2004003950

Facts On File books are available at special discounts when purchased in bulk quantities for businesses, associations, institutions, or sales promotions. Please call our Special Sales Department in New York at (212) 967-8800 or (800) 322-8755.

You can find Facts On File on the World Wide Web at http://www.factsonfile.com

Produced by the Shoreline Publishing Group LLC
Editorial Director: James Buckley Jr.
Series Editor: Beth Adelman
Designed by Thomas Carling, Carling Design, Inc.
Photo research by Jullie Chung, PhotoSearch, NY
Index by Word Co.

Photo and art credits: AP/Wide World Photos: 1, 16, 24, 34, 40, 54, 66, 96, 118; Giraudon/Art Resource, NY: 3, 21; Kozuyoshi Monachi/The Image Works 4; University of Edinburgh, Arabic and Persian Mss., no. 20.f.45b; Photofest: 12; Bibliothèque nationale de France. MS. Arabe 5847 f. 94v: 14; Mike Nelson/EPA-Photo: 24; Snark/Art Resource, NY: 32; Facts On File: 36, 117; Vanni/Art Resource, NY: 42; Bob Bull: 45, 100; Hideo Haga/HAGA/The Image Works: 47; Bibliothèque nationale de France. MS. Fr. 352 f. 49v: 50; The British Library: 57; Réunion de Musées Nationaux/Art Resource: 61; Tom Hollyman/Photo Researchers, Inc. 73; Art Resource, NY: 78; Bodleian Library, Oxford, MS. Marsh 144, page 273: 88; Erich Lessing/Art Resource, NY: 95; Bibliothèque nationale de France, MS. Arabe 6094 fol. 68: 102; Greg Niedermeiser/Bildarchiv Preussischer Kulturbesitz/Art Resource, NY: 109; Marcel Malherbe/Image Works: 114

Printed in the United States of America

VB PKG 10 9 8 7 6 5 4 3 2 1

This book is printed on acid-free paper.

CONTENTS

Introduction

FROM 632 TO 1258, THE ISLAMIC EMPIRE WAS THE MOST powerful and cultured domain in the world. Less than a century after its founding, it had grown from a loose confederation of desert tribes into the largest empire in the history of the world. No ancient empire extended its reach farther around the globe. At its height, the Islamic Empire stretched from Spain in the west to the borders of India in the east, from central Asia in the north to North Africa in the south. The Muslim conquests led to the downfall of one ancient empire and the devastation of another.

Throughout their newly conquered lands, the Muslims created a bond between the conquerors and the conquered through the religion of Islam and the Arabic language. As a result, the Islamic Empire left behind a religious, political, and cultural legacy that survives to this day. Philip K. Hitti, a professor of Arab history, wrote in *The Arabs: A Short History*, "Islam is a way of life that has religious aspects, political aspects, and cultural aspects, and each of the three overlaps and interacts."

Unlikely Beginnings

The Islamic Empire began in 632 in the hot, barren regions of the western Arabian Peninsula. This parched land was one-third desert, with few streams that flowed year round. The empire had its roots in a religious movement, started by a man named Muhammad (c. 570–632) who was born in Mecca, a city in modern-day Saudi Arabia. The laws of the empire were based on the messages Muhammad received from Allah (the Arabic word for God). People throughout the empire modeled their behavior on the moral teachings and the example set by Muhammad, whom Muslims consider the example of the most perfect life ever lived.

The Islamic Empire was at its height during what is known in Western history as the early Middle Ages. The early Middle Ages date from around the collapse of the Roman Empire in the late fourth century until the early 1100s. In Europe, this period was marked by a stagnation of ideas and culture, and for this reason, it is sometimes known as the Dark Ages. At the same time, however, lands under the control of the Muslims were experiencing a golden age of learning, commerce, and civilization. Many ideas that came out of Islamic lands laid the foundation for the European Renaissance in the 1400s.

Aging Kingdoms

By the early 400s, the once-mighty Roman Empire had broken into two distinct empires, West and East. Although the Western Roman Empire did not last for long, the Eastern Roman Empire developed into a powerful entity known as the Byzantine Empire. The Byzantine Empire included the Balkan Peninsula and Asia Minor. The Byzantines also conquered much of the Middle East, including Egypt, as well as North Africa.

The Byzantines had competition for control of the Middle East. The Sassanian, or Persian Empire dominated the areas to the southeast of Byzantium. The Sassanians ruled all of modern Iran and parts of Iraq, Pakistan, Afghanistan, Turkmenistan, Uzbekistan, and the Gulf Coast of the Arabian Peninsula.

These two powerful empires were very different from one another, in both culture and religion. While the Byzantine Empire was a Christian kingdom, the Sassanians followed Zoroastrianism—a Persian religion founded by the prophet and teacher Zoroaster (c. 630–c. 553 B.C.E.).

The two empires were constantly at war with one another. Many important trade routes between the empires and their desirable goods ran through the Arabian Peninsula. The region became a source of contention between the two empires. Both the Byzantines and the Sassanians wanted control of the trade routes to China and the spice-laden lands in the Indian Ocean. To pay for these wars, both empires placed heavy taxes on the citizens under their control. These taxes, along with other restrictions, caused unrest in Sassanian and Byzantine lands, especially among the Arab tribes living on the fringes of the two empires.

By the early 600s, the region was ripe for revolution. The constant warfare had left both empires weak and unable to keep a strong grip on the lands and peoples of the Middle East. And the Arabs themselves were ready for change.

The Arabian Peninsula Before Muhammad

In the early 600s, the Arabian Peninsula was a desert-like region with a few fertile areas on the edges. Towns, usually centered around a spring or well of fresh water, were few and far between. Most Arabs were Bedouin nomads who wandered from place to place in search of grazing land for their sheep. (Bedouin is an Arabic word that means "people of the desert.")

The Bedouins lived in tribes organized by blood relationships. To become stronger, groups of tribes, related by marriage or kinship, might band together to form a larger, more powerful unit. For the Bedouin, loyalty to one's tribe was of the utmost importance. Each tribe member depended upon the others to help them survive in the harsh desert environment. If a member of another tribe harmed or killed a tribe member, it was the duty of the injured person's tribe to right the wrong. The principle of blood vengeance was a key part of tribal life.

Life in the desert was difficult. The world the Bedouins lived in was hot, dry, and often hostile. Camels were an important part of their lives, and a major means of transportation—earning the animals the nickname "ships of the desert." They also provided sustenance and support for the Bedouins. The camel's hair was used to make tents and clothing, as was its hide. Camel manure was used as fuel, while its urine was used as a medicine, insect repellent, and shampoo. The Bedouins also ate camel meat to supplement their basic meal of dates and milk. According to historian Philip Hitti, the Arabic language may have as many as a thousand different words for the camel. The words describe camels of different breeds, conditions, and stages of growth.

Warfare between Bedouin tribes was constant. In the harsh desert environment, where water—or the lack of it—could mean the

Bedouins Today

Bedouin people continue to make their homes in the deserts of the Arabian Peninsula and North Africa today. As many as 6 million people still live a nomadic life. The head of a tribe is known as the *sheikh*. The title is not hereditary; following ancient tradition, the position is given to the most senior male member of the tribe.

As in the past, the Bedouins rely heavily on the one-humped dromedary camel. These hearty creatures store fat in their humps, and can go for up to six weeks with little food or water. They can also carry heavy loads, an important attribute to the nomadic Bedouins, and can walk as far as 100 miles in one day.

Bedouin camels are well-known for their swiftness. They can move at speeds of more than 10 miles per hour. In recent years, Bedouins have begun breeding camels in large numbers to sell to wealthy Arabs, who often use the camels for racing.

The Arabian Horse

Most horse lovers are familiar with a beautiful breed of horse known as the Arabian. The Arabian descended from horses that came to the Arabian Peninsula from North Africa and Mesopotamia (modern-day Iraq), and was probably the first domesticated breed of horse in the world. These animals were valued by wealthy Bedouins for their speed, beauty, and strength.

In the eighth century, the Arabian horse was brought to Spain during the Islamic conquest of that region. During the Crusades (see page 49), it was bred with English horses. Several breeds that are very common now have the Arabian horse as part of their "parental stock." These breeds include the Thoroughbred, American Saddle Horse, and Quarter Horse.

difference between life and death, clans often fought for control of the wells that dotted the region. Fertile grazing lands for camels and goats were also a source of conflict. Raids of other tribes and towns on the desert borders were common. During these raids, the Bedouins took camels and other needed supplies. Any goods that were not secured through raiding could later be purchased at the towns' marketplaces.

The Bedouin tribes looked down upon their neighbors who lived in the towns that dotted the western peninsula. For the townsfolk, life was easier and more settled. With the aid of reservoirs and irrigation, some areas were able to support farming. Here, they grew barley, wheat, melons, dates, and nuts. The business that proved the most important to the early towns, however, was trade. Major trade routes ran through the western peninsula, helping connect Africa and the Far East to the Mediterranean regions. Caravans of camels carried cloth, spices, and gemstones to Syria and Palestine. From these ports, the goods were then shipped to Europe.

The Arabs also produced some important products of their own. The top native commodities shipped to other parts of the world were perfumes and incense. The Arabs were especially known for frankincense and myrrh. These two scents, obtained from the gum of trees and shrubs, were highly prized in the great empires of Rome, Egypt, Persia, and Babylon. They were also very valuable: In the New Testament of the Bible, the baby Jesus is given gifts of gold, frankincense, and myrrh by the Three Wise Men.

Before Muhammad was born, there were three major towns on the Arabian Peninsula. All were located in the Hijaz, a mountainous region on the western coast. Yathrib, the northernmost town, was made up of farms and small villages settled around an oasis (an area in the desert that has water and vegetation). Taif was a mountain resort area, used by wealthy Arabs to escape the summer heat. Mecca, the third town, seemed to have the least potential for success. Located in a rocky area with little vegetation, Mecca was surrounded by mountains. By the early 600s, however, it was the wealthiest and most important town on the peninsula.

Mecca

Mecca was the commercial center of the Arabian Peninsula. A center of trade, the town was an important stop along many caravan routes between Syria, Iraq, southwestern Arabia, and the Red Sea. Mecca was also

CONNECTIONS >>>>>>>>>>>>>>>>>>>>>>>>>>>>>>

Coffee

The history of coffee is something of a mystery. Most experts believe that coffee was first grown in Africa, probably in Ethiopia. Some historians believe coffee had made its way to the Arabian Peninsula by about 675; others place its arrival there at around 1000. At the very latest, coffee was growing in Yemen by the 1400s. Even the source of the word coffee is up for debate. Some say the beverage takes its name from Kaffa, the Ethiopian province where coffee was first grown. Others say that it gets its name from an Arabic phrase once applied to wine, *al-qahwa*.

At first, coffee beans were chewed rather than ground, roasted, and turned into liquid. By end of the 15th century, however, coffee had become a popular drink throughout the Middle East. Coffeehouses, where men could meet and socialize while enjoying a cup of the strong beverage, soon sprang up. According to Bernard Lewis in *The Middle East: A Brief History of the Last 2,000 Years*, the coffeehouse served as the Middle East's equivalent of the tavern in Europe. Philip Hitti, in *History of the Arabs: From the Earliest Times to the Present*, calls coffee the "wine of Islam."

During the 16th century, the production and exportation of coffee from Yemen became an important part of Middle Eastern trade with Europe. Coffee quickly became as popular in Europe as it was in the Middle East, and in the early 1640s, the first European coffeehouse opened for business in Venice, Italy.

Coffee may have been brought to the United States in 1607, when Captain John Smith helped found the first permanent English settlement in Jamestown, Virginia. After the Boston Tea Party in 1773, coffee became the patriot's drink of choice. Today, coffee is still one of America's most popular beverages. In 2000, more than half of all American adults drank coffee daily, according to the National Coffee Association. Most coffee imported into the United States is a type called Arabian or Arabica coffee; however, most Arabian coffee today is grown in Central and South America.

the center of religion for most Arabs. Before Muhammad, Arabian tribes practiced animism, a type of worship that attributes supernatural powers to objects in nature. For example, stones, springs, or trees might be worshiped as sacred objects. The principle god of the Arab people was Allah. Allah was believed to be the creator of the universe, and was much stronger than the other gods.

Mecca was at the heart of this animistic worship. Each year, thousands of pilgrims made their way to Mecca to take part in religious festivals centered around the Kaaba, a large cube-shaped building in the middle of town. The Kaaba, a one-room structure made of dark stone and covered with a black cloth, was home to the sacred Black Stone. This stone, embedded in one of the walls, was believed to have been placed there originally by Adam, the first man, and later by the prophet Abraham (from whom the Arabs say they are descended). The Kaaba was also thought to be the home of the animistic god Hubal, and more than 300 other minor gods.

Although Mecca was a center of animistic worship, monotheism—the worship of one god—was also present. Groups of Jews and Christians lived throughout the region. The town of Yathrib, which would play an important role in the spread of Islam, was home to a large Jewish population.

Mecca was controlled by a wealthy tribe of merchants called the Quraysh, who had become rich by monopolizing the town's trading business. They then took control of the government, appointing only members of their own tribe to positions on the town's council. As the ruling tribe, the Quraysh also controlled the care and maintenance of the Kaaba.

Around the year 610, a Meccan named Muhammad, also a member of the Quraysh, received a revelation from God. Muhammad began preaching about this revelation, and soon attracted a number of followers. The new religion was called Islam, and the followers of Muhammad the Prophet were called Muslims. Over the years, many were attracted to Muhammad and his message, which included caring for poor people, living modestly, and adhering to a strict moral code. The Islamic religion grew. Upon Muhammad's death in 632, a real empire began to take shape. Islam's founder was both a political and religious leader, and in the empire that grew up after him religion and politics were so intertwined that they could not be separated. The law of the empire was the law of Islam, given to Muhammad by God.

Muhammad's successors quickly conquered surrounding areas and tribes. They moved throughout the region, taking control of lands on the

Arabian Peninsula, and then stretching into the Byzantine and Sassanian Empires. In less than 100 years, they held land on three different continents and had created the largest empire the world had yet seen.

Although the conquerors generally did not force their religion or culture on the conquered, the Islamic religion and the Arabic language spread to the lands they held. Many of the conquered people converted to Islam. Some converted to avoid paying a tax levied on non-Muslims, others out of a deep belief in the message of Muhammad. Because it was the language of the government, Arabic also spread. The Islamic Empire lasted for a little more than six centuries, and Islam and Arabic continued to have profound effect on the world, even into modern times.

Angelic Voice
This page from an illuminated book in Arabic and Persian (dates unknown) shows the angel Gabriel speaking to Muhammad.

The Legacy of the Empire

Today, modern connections to the ancient Islamic Empire can be found all around us: place names, words, cultural contributions, architecture, and medical, mathematical, and scientific innovations are just a few of the areas in which the contributions of the empire have been lasting. Although many of the things we consider to be "Arabic" were, in fact, borrowed from conquered peoples, the Muslims left their own unique mark on them.

The greatest legacy of the empire, however, is Islam, the last of the three great monotheistic religions. Although Islam is the world's youngest major religion, it currently has more followers than any other religion except Christianity. About 1.3 billion people around the globe are Muslims. It is also one of the fastest growing religions in the world.

Islam is a powerful political force in today's world. There are more than 50 countries in which Islam is the state religion, including Iran, Iraq, Pakistan, and Afghanistan. There are also large Muslim populations in many other countries, including Bangladesh, Indonesia, Israel, China, Russia, India, and a number of nations in Central Asia. Although the Islamic religion was born on the Arabian Peninsula, most Muslims today are not Arabs. Currently, between 15 percent and 20 percent of all Muslims are Arab.

In the United States, Muslims are an important minority. There are about 6 million Muslims in the United States. That number more than doubled from 1990. Large Muslim populations are found in Los Angeles, Detroit, and New York City. There are more than 1,200 mosques in the country, according to the Hartford Seminary.

CONNECTIONS >>>>>>>>>>>>>>>>>>>>>>>>>>>>>>>>>>

I Dream of Jinni

Many of the minor gods the Bedouins prayed to were forces of good. But there were also forces of mischief to be dealt with. And some spirits embodied both. The jinn were spirits capable of assuming human or animal form and exercising supernatural influence over people for good or for ill. The Bedouins believed they roamed the desert, causing trouble and spying on humans. However, some jinn also inspired tribal poets.

According to the Quran (sometimes written as *Koran*), jinn were created out of smokeless fire. One of the best-known jinn is Satan, cast from heaven by God because he refused to bow down to humans. The Quran states that after Muhammad began preaching, a group of jinn heard him and converted to Islam.

The singular of jinn is *jinni*, and in English this word is written as genie. The idea of genies was popularized in the West by the *Thousand and One Nights*, a collection of Arabian, Persian, and Indian folktales compiled over hundreds of years. The genie in the Disney Studios movie *Aladdin* is a far cry from the original jinn of the Bedouin world.

I Dream of Genie *was a popular television series in the 1970s that borrowed from the jinn legends.*

PART I

HISTORY

The Beginning of the Empire

The Empire at Its Largest

The Last Years of the Empire

وَكَادَ يَنْزِعُ الجِمَالَ الشَّمَّرَ وَأَنْشَدَ

مَا الحَجُّ سَيْرَكَ تَأْوِيبًا وَإِدْلَاجَا وَلَا الْغِيَامَ جِمَالًا وَأَحْدَاجَا

الحَجُّ أَنْ تَقْصِدَ الْبَيْتَ الْحَرَامَ عَلَى تَجْرِيدِكَ الْحَجَّ لَا تَبْغِي بِهِ حَاجَا

وَتَمْضِيَ كَأَهْلِ الْإِنْصَافِ مُتَّخِذًا رَدْعَ الْهَوَى هَادِيًا وَالْحَقَّ مِنْهَاجَا

CHAPTER 1

The Beginning of the Empire

THE SEEDS OF THE ISLAMIC EMPIRE WERE SOWN AROUND 570, when Muhammad ibn (son of) Abd Allah was born in Mecca. His father died before Muhammad was born. As was the custom, the small child was sent to a Bedouin family in the desert to be nursed, because Arabs believed that the desert provided a better, healthier environment for a child's growth.

Muhammad (whose name means "worthy of praise" in Arabic) returned to Mecca when he was still very young. But tragedy followed him. His mother died when he was just six, and his grandfather died soon after. Muhammad was left to be raised by his father's brother, Abu Talib (d. 619), one of the most prominent of the Quraysh in Mecca and a chief of the Hashemite tribe.

Despite his uncle's prominence, Muhammad himself was a poor orphan—something he never forgot. Later, as leader of a powerful political and religious entity, Muhammad was especially sympathetic to the poor, orphaned, and disadvantaged.

Like most young men of his time, Muhammad learned archery, horsemanship, swordplay, and the principles of trading. Under his uncle's guidance, he began leading trade caravans across the desert. He soon earned a reputation as a competent and honest businessman. Before long, people were calling him al-Amin, which means "the trustworthy."

When Muhammad was 25, he married Khadija (d. 620), the wealthy widow of a Meccan merchant, who was 15 years older than he. The two met when Muhammad began leading trading caravans for Khadija. Muhammad is said to have loved his wife, and their relationship was a strong one: Although polygamy (the practice of having more than one

Sacred Site
Modern pilgrims walk around the Kaaba during the final day of the hajj. The Kaaba stands at the heart of the Grand Mosque in Mecca, Saudi Arabia.

wife) was common among Arab men, Muhammad took no other wives for the 25 years he was married to Khadija. Together, the couple had at least six children, although Muhammad's two sons died when they were just infants. Of his four daughters, Fatima (c. 605–633), the oldest, was his favorite.

Even before he received his revelation from God, Muhammad displayed wisdom and diplomatic skills. When he was in his mid 30s, the Kaaba was damaged in a flood. As the leading Meccan tribe, the Quraysh were put in charge of rebuilding it. After the work had been done, however, the chief members of the tribe's different segments began arguing about who should have the privilege of placing the Black Stone back in its home. Muhammad solved the problem by having one man from each of the four groups who had worked on the Kaaba carry the stone together on a cloth. Muhammad himself placed the stone into the corner wall.

As he got older, Muhammad sought peace and solitude in a cave in the cliffs of Hira, a nearby mountain. Here he would meditate, and eventually began to see visions and hear someone speaking to him. In 610, Muhammad received a visit from the angel Gabriel, sent to him by God. Gabriel instructed him to make *quran*, or recite the word of God. Terrified and confused, Muhammad fled for home. But on the way, Gabriel confronted him again, saying, "O Muhammad, you are the Apostle of God." At first, Muhammad thought he might be losing his sanity. The visitations stopped. But a year later, he received another message. Muhammad then embraced his role as God's prophet and opened himself up to the messages. Over the next 20 years, he continued to receive revelations from God.

Three years after receiving his first message, Muhammad began preaching what had been revealed to him. After his death, these

CONNECTIONS >>>>>>>>>>>>>>>>>>>>>>>>>>>>>>

The Kaaba Today

Rebuilt many times throughout the centuries, the Kaaba today is a cubic structure about 50 feet tall, enclosed by the Grand Mosque of Mecca. Two of the Kaaba's walls measure about 40 feet long, while the other two walls are about 35 feet long. The area around the Kaaba can hold hundreds of thousands of worshipers at one time. One of the most recent additions is a solid gold gate.

The black silk cloth that covers the Kaaba is decorated with black calligraphy patterns. Passages from the Quran are embroidered on the cloth with gold thread. Each year, a new cloth is made to be draped over the Kaaba.

The Black Stone lies embedded in the southeast corner of the Kaaba. The stone, which may be a meteorite, measures 11 inches wide and 15 inches high. Over the years, the stone has broken into several pieces and it is now surrounded by a silver frame to hold it together. In the corner opposite the Black Stone lies a reddish stone, called the Stone of Felicity.

The Kaaba is the focal point of all Muslim prayers to Mecca. Within the Kaaba, people can face in any direction when they pray. Outside the Kaaba, all Muslims face it to pray—no matter where they are in the world. A 12-mile area around the Kaaba is declared *haram*, or restricted. Only Muslims are allowed to enter this area, and, as a sacred site, the spilling of blood and other profane actions are prohibited.

Each year, thousands of Muslims travel to the Kaaba, the end point of the *hajj* (pilgrimage) that all Muslims who can afford it are required to make at least once in their lives. The pilgrims circle the Kaaba and kiss the Black Stone. It is important to remember, however, that the Black Stone itself is not an object of worship. Pilgrims are simply following the tradition set by Muhammad himself.

revelations were collected into the Quran. This holy scripture of Islam provided the laws and regulations by which the new community gathering around his teachings was to live and work.

Muhammad preached that there was only one God, Allah, and that all must surrender to his will and worship only him. Muhammad's new religion eventually became known as Islam, from the Arab word for

The Basics of Islam

Before Islam, the Arabs worshiped a number of gods and idols. They also worshiped stones, trees, and wells, and worshiped them—a belief called *animism*. However, the Arabs still recognized a main god, whom they called Allah.

Islam, as the youngest monotheistic (belief in one god) religion, appeared centuries after Judaism and Christianity. Muhammad admired the Bible, and many stories from the Old Testament are mentioned in the Quran, as is Jesus. Muslims recognize a number of Biblical figures as the prophets of God, including Adam, Abraham, Moses, and Jesus. As God's messengers, they are all respected and honored by Muslims, as is Mary, Jesus' mother. Jesus is not, however, recognized as divine. Muslims do not believe Muhammad was divine either. Rather, he was God's final prophet—a carrier of God's divine message and the living example of how to lead a pious and good life. The Islamic religion believes that there is only one God, and that is Allah.

The Five Pillars of Islam, or *arkan al-Islam*, are the five fundamental actions that should be performed by all Muslims, no matter what branch of Islam they follow. They are:

1. Profession of belief. That is, belief in one God, Allah. To do this, Muslims repeat a phrase known as the *shahada*: "There is no God but Allah and Muhammad is His Prophet."

2. Prayer. Muslims pray five times a day, at fixed times. These daily prayers are known together as *salat*.

3. Almsgiving. During the early days of the empire, the Muslims developed two types of tithes, or religious taxes: a voluntary tithe, or *sadaqa*, and a mandatory tithe, or *zakat*. The *zakat* was used to provide for widows, orphans, and the poor. It could also be used to ransom captives, help slaves buy their freedom, and equip volunteers for jihad. Today, the *zakat* is 2.5 percent of one's liquid assets and income-generating properties. Shiites also pay an additional tithe of 20 percent on all new income.

4. Fasting. During the month of Ramadan (the ninth month of the Islamic calendar), Muslims must abstain from food, drink, and sexual relations from dawn to sunset each day. This fasting is known as *saum*.

5. Pilgrimage. All Muslims should make a journey to Mecca at least once in their lifetime during the *hajj*, or time of pilgrimage. The hajj occurs during the first 10 days of Dhul-Hijjah (the 12th month of the Islamic calendar.)

submission. His followers were called Muslims, or "those who surrender." The Quran also laid out prayer schedules, marriage and divorce laws, and rules for the treatment of slaves, prisoners of war, enemies, and orphans.

At first, Muhammad's followers consisted of close family and a few friends. Slowly, however, the little group grew. Because the teachings of the Quran included the equality of all people and charity to the poor, it was very attractive to the underprivileged of Mecca. The new religion also gave followers the hope of an afterlife, where they would be judged for their worldly deeds. Those who lived by God's word would go to heaven, while those who had sinned would spend eternity in hell.

Muhammad attacked idol worship, an important money-making industry for Mecca. His messages of equality and the duty to care for the underprivileged angered the wealthy merchants. Not only was Muhammad threatening the importance of the Quraysh, he was attacking ancient tribal ways of life by preaching that God should be placed before tribal ties. The Quraysh began harassing him and his followers. Muslims were at first greeted with jeers and ridicule. When this failed to dissuade them from their faith, the attacks on Muhammad and his followers turned violent. In one case, a slave who had converted to Islam was placed in the burning desert sun with stones on his chest and left to die. One of Muhammad's stepsons was stoned and killed while praying at the Kaaba. Armed skirmishes between Muslims and the Quraysh became common. To escape the violence, some of Muhammad's followers fled from Mecca to Ethiopia, in northeastern Africa.

In a final attempt to quiet Muhammad and diminish his influence, the Quraysh refused to allow him to worship at the Kaaba. Then Muhammad's uncle died in 619, and other members of his clan withdrew their protection from him. These events placed Muhammad in serious danger.

He began searching for a town that would welcome him and his followers. He first turned to Taif, the thriving farming town south of Mecca. Because some members of Muhammad's clan made their homes here, he expected a welcome. But instead of offering sanctuary, clan members drove Muhammad from town.

Muhammad was finally successful in the town of Yathrib, already home to a number of Muslim converts. The people welcomed him as a mediator and problem-solver, and in 622 his followers began the journey to Yathrib. Muhammad, along with his friend and father-in-law Abu Bakr (573–634), was one of the last to leave. Learning of a plot to kill

Muhammad, the two men fled from Mecca in the dead of night. The journey to Yathrib is known as the Hijra, or "migration," and is an important event in Islamic history. The Hijra is considered the official birth of the Islamic religion. It is also considered the birth of the Umma, the Muslim community, and the beginning of the Muslim calendar.

Yathrib was eventually renamed Medina, from the Arabic *madinat al-nabi*, or "City of the Prophet." Muhammad's time in Medina is called the Medinan period, and it saw the flowering of the Umma—a community based on a shared religion, not on kinship and blood ties.

During his 10 years in Medina, Muhammad became more than just a spiritual leader. He put his administrative and political skills to good use, effectively acting as the town's leader. All of the legal and political decisions in Medina reflected the words of God as revealed through Muhammad. Muhammad's power also improved the lot of Muslims in the town. While they had been spit at and vilified in Mecca, in Medina they had prestige and importance. Islam was evolving from a religious movement to a powerful political one.

First Battles

To help support his new community, Muhammad and the Muslims soon began raiding trading caravans making their way to and from Mecca. The Muslims practiced the Arab custom of the raid, or *razzia*. In the book *Muhammad: Prophet and Statesman*, W. Montgomery Watt says the raid was "a normal feature of Arab desert life. It was a kind of sport rather than war." The attackers would surprise their victims, take what they wanted, then disappear again. Hand-to-hand combat was rare. During the raids, the Muslims took both goods and hostages, wreaking havoc on Mecca's economy.

Muhammad said he had received a message from God concerning the rightness of these actions. The Quran (chapter 22, verse 39) states, "Permission to take up arms is hereby given to those who are attacked, because they have been wronged." Because Muhammad and his followers had been attacked in Mecca, they believed the raids were justified as a way of fighting back.

The Quraysh were, of course, alarmed by the raids. They believed that when Muhammad left Mecca, they had seen the last of him. But trade was their lifeblood, and they would not tolerate its disruption. In 624, Muhammad led about 315 Muslims from Medina to Badr, a stopover for trade caravans located 90 miles south of Medina. Here, they waited to

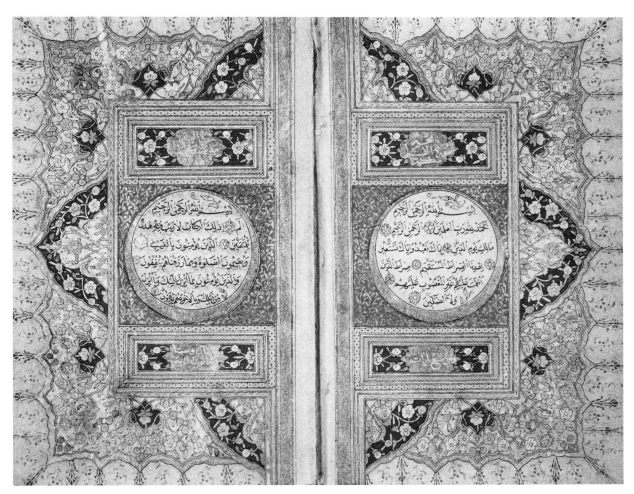

ambush a large caravan they knew would be passing through. However, word of the ambush got back to Mecca. The Quraysh were determined to wipe out the troublesome Muslims, and sent nearly 1,000 men to punish Muhammad and his followers.

The Battle of Badr began with several warriors from each side challenging one another to single combat. This was an ancient Arab custom. After the single combat, the Muslim troops raced into battle, shouting the battle cry, *"Allahu Akbar!"* ("God is most great!"). The men fought hard using swords, bows, and arrows. Although the Muslims were outnumbered three to one and were poorly armed and lacked experience, they were disciplined and unafraid to die. Before the battle, Muhammad promised his warriors that anyone who died fighting for Islam that day would immediately enter paradise. To the surprise of many, the Muslims

Illuminating the Word
This page from a Turkish edition of the Quran (date unknown) is beautifully decorated. Illuminating the Quran was considered an act of worship.

21

Facing Mecca

Today, Muslims around the world turn their faces toward Mecca when they pray. In every mosque, one can find a *mihrab*, or niche, that indicates in which direction the faithful should pray. Above many *mihrabs* are the words Muhammad received in revelation (as recorded in the Quran): "Many a time have we seen you turn your face toward the sky. We will make you turn toward a *qiblah* [direction] that will please you. Turn your face toward the Holy Mosque [the Kaaba in Mecca]; wherever you be, turn your faces toward it."

emerged victorious. After the victory, Muhammad would not allow his men to slaughter the enemy captives, as was the custom of the time.

Muhammad's victory was seen by his followers as a sign from God that the Muslim raids were just and right. One of Allah's messages to Muhammad, as recorded in the Quran (chapter 21, verse 105), was, "The righteous among My servants shall inherit the earth." After the Battle of Badr, Bedouin tribes flocked to Medina to offer their allegiance to Muhammad. The Bedouins were known as fierce fighters, on horseback and on foot, and their presence attracted even more tribes, who journeyed to Medina to offer their support or pledge peace.

After the Battle of Badr, tensions between Muhammad and the Jews of Medina came to a head. Some of this contention was political and some religious. The Jews did not recognize Muhammad's claim to be a prophet in the line of the ancient Jewish prophets. And the Muslims accused them of supporting the Meccans. One of Medina's Jewish tribes was forced to leave the town, and the Muslims confiscated the property of everyone who fled. Later, a second tribe was expelled. Finally, in 627, Muhammad accused the remaining Jews of cooperating with the enemy Meccans. About 600 Jewish men were beheaded, and the women and children were sold into slavery.

After their humiliating defeat at Badr, the Meccans prepared to try again. In 625, they sent 3,000 men to attack the Muslims outside Medina. At the Battle of Uhud, Muhammad himself was wounded and the Muslims were overpowered and forced to retreat. However, the Meccans were not able to capture Medina itself.

Over the next three years, dozens of battles took place between the Meccans and the Muslims in Medina. Muhammad himself led about 20 of these battles. Finally, in 628, Muhammad negotiated a truce with the Meccans and in the following year returned as a pilgrim to the city's holy sites. The murder of one of his followers provoked him to attack the city, which soon surrendered. Muhammad acted generously to the Meccans, demanding only that the pagan idols around the Kaaba be destroyed. "Truth has come and falsehood has vanished," he said. Muhammad declared that the area around the Kaaba was now a sanctuary, a holy place to the One God, Allah. Mecca was a Muslim city.

Muhammad dealt leniently with the Meccans, particularly the Quraysh, awarding them positions of authority and power. It was a shrewd move—soon the Quraysh were helping Muhammad abolish idolatry and subdue area tribes. The Muslims sent troops out to the surrounding areas to destroy animistic temples. With that kind of persuasion, the number of converts to Islam grew rapidly.

Muhammad's Successors

In early 632, Muhammad made another journey from Medina to Mecca. Long gone were the days when only his family and closest friends followed his teachings. On this pilgrimage, called the hajj, Muhammad was accompanied by 30,000 of his followers. During the hajj, pilgrims had to follow strict rules of behavior. There was to be no violence, no sexual intercourse, no arguing or ill will.

Upon his arrival in Mecca, Muhammad began a ritual that modern-day pilgrims continue to follow. He circled the Kaaba seven times. Then he kissed and touched the Black Stone. Other parts of Muhammad's ritual included going back and forth between two hills seven times, throwing pebbles at three pillars representing Satan, and slaughtering sheep to commemorate Abraham's willingness to sacrifice his son Ishmael to God. (In the Jewish and Christian bibles, Isaac is the son God asks Abraham to sacrifice; Muslims disagree with this version of events.)

The first hajj, often called the Farewell Pilgrimage, was Muhammad's last trip to Mecca. He seemed to know that his life was coming to an end. Preaching a sermon on the plain of Arafat, Muhammad told his followers, "I do not know whether I shall ever meet you in this place again."

A few months after returning to Medina, Muhammad became ill and died. At the time of his death, he was the most powerful political and religious leader in the region. In just 20 years, he had conquered or won over most of the tribes on the Arabian Peninsula. He had destroyed animism and idol worship, replacing these practices with a strong new monotheistic religion. Perhaps most importantly, he had inaugurated a new way of life for the community of Muslims.

IDOLS AND ISLAMIC ART

When Muhammad destroyed the idols in Mecca, he set in motion an artistic style that continues to this day. Figurative art, in which humans are depicted, is prohibited in mosques and on materials used for worship. Islamic art generally makes use of geometric shapes and calligraphy rather than representational forms.

Muhammad's status was such that, at first, many of his followers refused to believe he was dead; some maintained that he would return. Abu Bakr, Muhammad's father-in-law and companion, finally spoke to the grieving Muslims. "If you worshiped Muhammad, know that he is dead," he said. "But if you worship the One God, know that he is alive and does not die."

Upon the death of Muhammad, a serious question arose that had the potential to create a crisis for the young religion: Should there be one leader or many to replace Muhammad as the religious and political leader of the Umma? And who, exactly, should take the great prophet's place as leader of the Arab people? Muhammad had been the absolute ruler of the Islamic community, but he had not designated a successor.

Two groups emerged with very different opinions on the matter. One group believed Muhammad had selected his son-in-law and cousin, Ali (d. 661), to be the caliph, or successor, after his death. Ali was married to Muhammad's favorite daughter, Fatima, and was one of the first to

The Prophet's Mosque
Muslim pilgrims relax outside the Prophet Muhammad's Mosque in Medina, Saudi Arabia. Muhammad's remains are buried in the mosque, and it is an important site in the hajj.

accept Islam. The group who believed in Ali's claim became known as the Shia, or "party of" Ali, also known as Shiites.

The second—and larger—group did not believe Muhammad had named any particular person to take his place. They chose to follow Arab tribal custom and allow the senior men of the Umma to choose the next ruler. The men decided Muhammad's successor should be selected from a group of his oldest and most faithful companions. After much discussion, they chose Abu Bakr. Those who supported Abu Bakr became known as the people of the Sunna (the traditions and examples of the Prophet) or Sunnis. (Today, about 88 percent of all Muslims are Sunni, while 11 percent are Shiite, according to the web site www.adherents.com.)

In the midst of much controversy, Abu Bakr became the first caliph. He was the first of four of Muhammad's companions who would eventually rule the early Islamic Empire. These first four leaders are known collectively as the "rightly guided" caliphs.

The first four caliphs were the most connected to the Umma. They were in charge of the political and religious life of the Muslim community, and they directed the raids and wars that led to the expansion of the empire. Although all four had been companions of Muhammad, none reigned without problems or dissent. Only Abu Bakr died a natural death. The last three were murdered.

Conquest Begins

After being selected caliph, Abu Bakr chose Medina as his capital. A wise and pious man, Abu Bakr had the support of the inhabitants of Mecca and Medina, as well as some of the area tribes. Still other tribes, however, had broken away from Islam upon the death of Muhammad. Many felt that they had pledged loyalty and obedience to Muhammad the leader, not to Islam the religion.

Abu Bakr moved swiftly to conquer these defecting tribes and bring them back into the fold of Islam. He placed Khalid ibn al-Walid (d. 642), known as the Sword of Islam, in charge of the fighting. Khalid was a great military leader and a brilliant strategist. Historian Philip Hitti calls his campaigns "among the most brilliantly executed in the history of warfare."

Khalid began by molding the fragmented Muslim troops, made up of volunteers from various tribes, into a unified, formidable fighting machine. The army was broken down into divisions, each with an assigned place on the battlefield, including a center, two wings, a vanguard, and a

COMMANDER OF THE FAITHFUL

Today, Morocco's King Mohammed VI (b. 1963) claims the title Commander of the Faithful. King Mohammed, the religious and political leader of the North African country, claims to be a direct descendant of the prophet Muhammad. The kings of Morocco have claimed this title since the 16th century, although it is not recognized by Muslims outside of Morocco.

Another claimant to the title of Commander of the Faithful is Omar Mohammed, Supreme Leader of the Taliban, the political party that controlled most of Afghanistan from 1996 to 2001. Omar took the title of Commander of the Faithful in 1996, but was not recognized as such by Muslims outside Afghanistan.

rear guard. Tribesmen fought together within these divisions. Each tribe had its own banner, which was carried into battle attached to a lance.

The general excelled in the surprise attack. With lightning speed, he would ride out of the desert on horseback, his cavalry behind him on horses and camels. He trained his cavalry in the use of the lance, which soon became one of the most feared weapons in the world when wielded by a Muslim soldier.

Backing up the cavalry was the infantry—soldiers on foot and armed with bows and arrows, slings, and swords. To protect themselves, the Muslim soldiers wore a light coat of mail (interlocking metal links) and carried a shield.

The battles to bring the rebellious tribes under control are known as the Ridda wars. Ridda is an Arabic word that means a defection from religion. As the tribes were subdued, they once again gave their loyalty to Islam and the new caliph. As a result, the number of troops fighting for Islam swelled. This marked the beginning of the first standing Islamic army.

By the time he died in 634, Abu Bakr had united the entire Arabian Peninsula under the banner of Islam. He had also begun raiding parts of Syria and Iraq—regions controlled by the Byzantine and Sassanian empires. Before his death, Abu Bakr picked Umar ibn al-Khattab (c. 581–644) as his successor, the second "rightly guided" caliph. Umar, like Abu Bakr, had been one of Muhammad's closest companions. Umar was the first caliph to use the title Commander of the Faithful. All future caliphs would also claim this title.

Tall and energetic, intelligent and just, Umar chose a simple lifestyle even when the riches of conquered kingdoms were in his hands. He ruled for 10 years, gaining a reputation as a man of wisdom and honor. He was responsible for introducing Islamic law and administrative functions to the conquered territories. He was especially noted for his piety. Umar carefully followed the laws of Islam. He even had his own son flogged to death for drunkenness and immoral behavior.

Umar quickly picked up where his predecessor had left off. Under Umar's command, Islamic troops continued their advance into neighboring regions controlled by the Byzantine and Sassanian Empires. The advances were a result of a coordinated strategy between the caliph, his officials, and the commanders of the armies of Medina, Mecca, and Taif.

From Medina, Umar sent troops to what is now the central Middle East. Before long, the Byzantine regions of Syria, Palestine, and Egypt were all in Muslim hands. Although the Byzantine ruler sent forces to oppose the invading troops, the Muslims had a huge advantage: knowledge of the desert. Arabian troops knew how to survive in the harsh environment. Their opponents did not. Safe in the dry, hostile land, the Islamic generals ordered their troops to wait until the enemy believed the threat of attack had passed. Then the Muslims would fly from the desert, attack, and conquer.

Khalid himself was a master of desert warfare. In early 635, Umar ordered his greatest general to make a 200-mile march across the desert to attack Damascus, the capital of Syria and a stronghold of the Byzantine Empire. According to legend, Khalid took camels that had gorged themselves with water. The general periodically ordered these camels to be killed so that the horses could drink the water stored in their stomachs and the men could eat their meat. After a six-month siege, Khalid and his men eventually took control of Damascus.

Khalid continued the practice of leniency to the conquered that Muhammad had shown during his lifetime. Before entering Damascus, the general promised the city's residents that they would be safe and that their city would not be destroyed. Khalid also promised that Muslim soldiers would not be lodged in their homes. He guaranteed that, as long as the people of Damascus paid the tax required by the caliph, they had nothing to fear.

As they advanced through the rest of the Byzantine Empire, Muslim troops encountered little resistance. In many cases, the conquered people welcomed the invaders with open arms and even cooperated with the Muslim attackers. Many were unhappy with the harsh Byzantine rule, and there is evidence that even some Christian sects that deviated from orthodox Christian doctrine were persecuted by the Byzantines. Other towns surrendered rather than face the fierce Arab fighters they had heard about.

These conquests were known as *jihad*, or "holy wars." Many Muslims saw the battles as efforts to fight evil and spread the message of Muhammad and the idea of monotheism. Those who died on the battlefield were considered to be martyrs who won a place in heaven by their death on behalf of Islam.

There were other, more material reasons for the conquests as well. The Arabian Peninsula was a desert with little vegetation or water. The inhabitants needed food and supplies, which they found in plentiful supply in the lands they conquered. These regions were some of the most

UNDER SIEGE
Siege warfare, although new to the Muslims, was an important battle strategy in the Middle Ages. During a siege, attackers prevented supplies and people from entering or exiting the city. The attackers might also use battering rams and other weapons to weaken the city's walls. Sieges could drag on for months—essentially starving the citizens of the town into surrender.

fertile areas in the world. But Muslim soldiers also found much more. Used to a simple, hard desert life, Arabian tribes were astonished by the wealth and riches of the cities they conquered. Being a soldier for the Islamic Empire became a lucrative and much desired profession. Arabs who survived the almost constant battles and attacks got rich; those who were killed while fighting to spread Islam earned a place in Paradise.

At the same time they were wreaking havoc in Byzantine regions, Muslim armies were chipping away at the Sassanian Empire. To defeat the weakened kingdom, Umar chose Saad ibn Abi Waqqas (d. 674) to lead the jihad. Saad was well-known to all Muslims. A close companion of Muhammad, he was said to have shed the first blood in defense of Islam back in Mecca before the Hijra. A seasoned warrior at the age of 40, Saad had also fought by Muhammad's side at the Battle of Badr. As a result, Muhammad had promised Saad that he, along with nine others, was assured a place in Paradise.

In 637, Saad and his troops made camp across the Euphrates River near Kadisiya in southern Iraq. The general sent representatives to the court of the Sassanian king, who turned them away and ordered his troops to cross the Euphrates River and attack them. Before the battle, parts of the Quran were recited. Then a number of soldiers from both sides engaged in single combat.

In the Sassanians, the Muslims met a very different enemy than any they had faced before. The Persians had 33 Asian elephants carrying on their backs *howdahs* (carts) filled with soldiers. From here, the soldiers could safely chuck spears at their Muslim opponents.

The battle raged until nightfall, when both sides retreated for the night. That evening, the Muslim troops danced and recited poetry—ancient tales of Arab bravery and victories. The following day, the battle resumed. This time, the Muslims had reinforcements and the Sassanians had left their elephants at home. To spook the Persians' horses, the Muslims rode camels covered with hoods and other cloths. After the second day of fighting, however, neither side could claim victory.

After battling a third day without any decisive winner, some of the Bedouin tribes decided to take matters into their own hands. That evening, they launched an attack on the Sassanian army that came to be called the Night of Fury. Fighting continued into dawn, until some Muslim soldiers broke through Sassanian lines and killed their general. The remaining Sassanian troops fled. Many died while trying to escape, either killed by Muslim soldiers or drowned while trying to cross the Euphrates.

The hard-fought victory left the Sassanian Empire wide open, and Saad and his troops soon conquered the old empire's capital, Ctesiphon (20 miles southeast of modern Baghdad in Iraq). Here, the general took up residence in the former king's royal palace, converting part of it into a mosque. He also confiscated the rest of the king's and his followers' property.

By the mid 650s, the Muslims had conquered a vast area that included the whole Arabian Peninsula, parts of North Africa, chunks of the Byzantine Empire, and most of the Sassanian Empire. They had even reached the borders of India. From their new lands, the troops continued their assault into the surrounding regions, pushing onward in their quest for more land and riches.

And riches they found, especially in such cities as Damascus, Alexandria, and Ctesiphon. The Arabs, used to an austere, simple way of life, were amazed by the opulent royal palaces and the wide variety of exotic goods they seized. One precious commodity, previously unknown to many of the invaders, was gold. Some soldiers even traded their share of gold for silver because they did not realize the metal's value.

One conquest that was especially important to the Muslims was the capture of Jerusalem from the Byzantine Empire in 637. All three of the great monotheistic religions thought of Jerusalem as a holy city. For Jews, it is the city of David (d. c. 970 B.C.E.) and Solomon (c. 974–c. 922 B.C.E.), Israel's two greatest kings, and the site of the original Temple. For Christians, it is the place of Jesus' crucifixion, his tomb, and his resurrection. Muslims believe Muhammad was transported to heaven from Jerusalem to hear the word of God before being returned to Mecca. After Mecca and Medina, Jerusalem is the third holiest city for Muslims. The Muslims controlled Jerusalem for most of the next 1,300 years.

The Dome of the Rock

The Dome of the Rock in Jerusalem is one of the many beautiful mosques built during the Islamic Empire. The mosque was built to protect the rock from which Muhammad ascended to heaven—the same rock on which Muslims believe Abraham prepared to sacrifice his son Ishmael, at God's command. Built on the site of the Temple of Solomon, the dome was commissioned by Caliph Abd al-Malik (c. 646–705) in 691.

Today, the Dome of the Rock remains one of the most distinctive and beautiful structures in Jerusalem. The most striking feature of the mosque is the large, shimmering golden dome, which towers over the city and is a distinctive landmark. Marble columns and archways, colorful mosaics, and intricately detailed calligraphy decorate the walls and ceilings.

Trouble Within

Umar was killed in 644 by a Persian Christian slave, stabbed with a poisoned dagger as he said morning prayers in the mosque. Uthman ibn Affan (c. 574–656), a member of Mecca's important Quraysh family and Muhammad's son-in-law, was chosen to replace him as the third rightly guided caliph. During his 12 years as caliph, Uthman continued the conquests that the two caliphs before him had begun. The Islamic Empire extended north as far as the Caucasus Mountains in southeastern Europe. He pushed further into North Africa and finished off the Sassanian Empire to the east.

Uthman, known as "the unpopular," was the first caliph who did not enjoy the widespread support of the Muslim community. Soon after taking power, the riches and wealth from the conquests began to dwindle and he began to lose popularity among the Arab soldiers. He lost even more support when he awarded conquered lands to members of his own family and those of his favorites. Uthman alienated other Muslims by appointing members of his family to important positions, taking money from the conquests, and acting in ways that many felt were not fitting for the leader of the Umma.

Armed revolts soon sprang up against the caliph. In 656, Uthman was murdered by a group of disgruntled Muslim soldiers while he was reading the Quran. This was the first time a caliph had been killed by other Muslims, and it set a bloody and dangerous precedent.

The murder of Uthman sparked the First Civil War, which lasted from 656 to 661. During the war, known in Arabic as *fitna*, which means "time of trial," the most important Muslim families struggled for control of the growing empire. One of those groups supported Ali, Muhammad's cousin and son-in-law and the fourth caliph. Ali had a close blood link to Muhammad–closer even than the first three caliphs. He had also been one of the original converts to Islam and had the support of most of the people of Medina and others in his party. They believed he should have been the first caliph and that the time had come to give him the title he deserved.

However, many people–especially the Umayyad family, Uthman's relatives–held Ali responsible for the third caliph's murder and did not think him worthy of being the caliph. The leader of the Umayyad opposition was Muawiya (602–680), governor of Damascus and a relative of the slain Uthman. Other prominent opponents included two early followers of Muhammad, and Muhammad's favorite wife in later years, Aisha (613–678).

Ali's opponents came to blows with the new caliph near Basra in southern Iraq. Here they were defeated at the Battle of the Camel in 656. During the battle, Aisha sat on the back of a camel in the midst of the fighting, urging her army to victory. The Battle of the Camel marked the first time Muslims took up arms against one another. It would not be the last.

After his victory, Ali moved the capital of the empire from Medina to Kufa, a garrison town in Iraq. In 657, just one year after defeating Aisha, Ali and his troops traveled north to Syria to attack Muawiya. But after a few skirmishes, Ali and Muawiya decided the conflict should be resolved through arbitration. Some of Ali's Shiite supporters did not agree. Their battle cry, "Only God has the right to decide," reflected their belief that right or wrong must be decided on the battlefield. They believed that God would support those who deserved victory. This group of Shiites left Ali in Kufa. They became known as the Kharijites, or seceders. The Kharijites believed that only those who did not sin could truly be Muslims. This belief lead them to oppose many later caliphs.

Ali was furious at the betrayal of the Kharijites and chased them to eastern Iraq, where his troops massacred many of them. His revenge against his former supporters further eroded his support among many Muslims.

Ali ruled for five stormy, war-torn years. Throughout his reign, problems within the Muslim community grew and deepened. In 661, Ali was murdered in the Kufa mosque when a Kharijite assassin stabbed him with a poisoned dagger. His death marked a split among Muslims throughout the empire.

CHAPTER 2

The Empire at Its Largest

IN 660 (A YEAR BEFORE THE DEATH OF ALI, THE FOURTH rightly guided caliph), Muawiya had himself proclaimed caliph in Jerusalem. A year later, when Ali was killed, Muawiya took complete control of the empire. He became the first ruler of the Umayyad Dynasty—named for the Umayyad family. Ironically, Muawiya's father had led the opposition to Muhammad in Mecca many years before. However, he later converted to Islam, and the intelligent and literate Muawiya had served as Muhammad's secretary.

Muawiya ruled the Islamic Empire capably for 20 years. He maintained a strong, stable government and was actively involved in the business of governing his huge empire. He oversaw taxation, the army, and new conquests. He also was the first caliph to mint Muslim coins for the empire, both gold and silver.

An important part of Muawiya's success was his selection of strong governors to control conquered lands throughout the empire. He chose capable men, often from his own family or clan, to be the chief administrators of the various regions. The new caliph was also a clever diplomat. His motto was, "I apply not my sword when my lash suffices, nor my lash when my tongue is enough," (quoted in Philip K. Hitti's *The Arabs: A Short History*). Muawiya was not adverse to using force when necessary, however. The caliph knew that the best way to keep restless soldiers from becoming rebellious was to keep them busy conquering new lands. Under his reign, the empire expanded dramatically.

As former governor of Damascus, the new caliph chose to make that city his capital. Damascus had been one of the first major cities to be captured by the Muslims, falling to Islamic troops in 635. Under Muawiya

OPPOSITE

Noble Young Man
Caliph Harun al-Rashid was the second ruler of the Abbasid Dynasty. He is shown as a young man in this 17th-century miniature painting from India, by Behzad.

33

Downtown Damascus
Pedestrians in downtown Damascus pass a billboard announcing the arrival of fast food chain Kentucky Fried Chicken. Just as during the Islamic Empire, modern Damascus is a brisk, busy city.

and later Umayyad caliphs, Damascus was transformed into a vibrant and thriving capital city. Over the years, it would come to be known as the "pearl of the east" and the "city of many pillars." Despite the beauty and culture of Damascus, Muawiya's decision to relocate the capital was controversial. Many Muslims believed Medina, the city of Muhammad, was the true heart of the empire.

For nearly a century, the Umayyads controlled the Islamic Empire from Damascus. During their reign, the empire grew to its largest size. Beginning with Muawiya, the Muslims expanded their conquests further into North Africa, Western Europe, and Central Asia. By the time the Umayyads were finished, the empire stretched across three continents, from the Atlantic Ocean to the Indus River Valley in what is now Pakistan.

Despite the expansion of the empire and the prosperity that went along with it, the reign of the Umayyad rulers was not a smooth one. The Shiites did not support the dynasty, and continued to believe that the descendants of Muhammad, through the fourth rightly guided caliph, Ali, should be the leaders of Islam. They created the title of *imam* to honor the male descendants of Muhammad, and the imams were their true spiritual and political leaders, not the caliphs. (Not every descendent of Muhammad was an imam, but only a certain line, and each imam was specifically designated by his predecessor.)

The Umayyad Dynasty

Before Muawiya's death, he arranged for his son Yazid to succeed him. To many Muslims, this action was shocking. Previously, caliphs were chosen by respected leaders of the community. By designating his son to follow in his footsteps, Muawiya was founding a royal dynasty.

Upon Muawiya's death in 680, the Second Civil War broke out. Conquest of other lands screeched to a halt as supporters of Muawiya's descendants battled supporters of Ali's descendants. The Umayyads, of course, supported Yazid (d. 683) as the rightful heir to the throne. When Yazid died just three years after his father, another Umayyad relative, Abd al-Malik ibn Marwan (647–705), was put forth as the next caliph.

The Shiites had a different caliph in mind, however. They put forth Ali's son, al-Husayn (627–680). In 680, Husayn led the Shiites in battle against Yazid at Karbala in Iraq. The Umayyads and their troops massacred Husayn, his family, and followers. Only two of Husayn's children escaped the slaughter. The event marked the permanent separation between the Shiites and Sunnis.

The Shiites were not the only ones who were dissatisfied with the Umayyad Dynasty. Many Muslims felt that the Umayyads were too "royal," and that this was not compatible with the teachings of Muhammad. One

CONNECTIONS >>>>>>>>>>>>>>>

Silk and Steel

During the Umayyad Dynasty, the capital city of Damascus was an important trade center. The capital was famous for damask, a type of silk cloth embroidered with intricate patterns. Another trademark craft of the city was damascened steel sword blades. Damascened steel has been etched or inlaid with wavy patterns of silver or gold. Damask silk and damascened steel are still highly prized today.

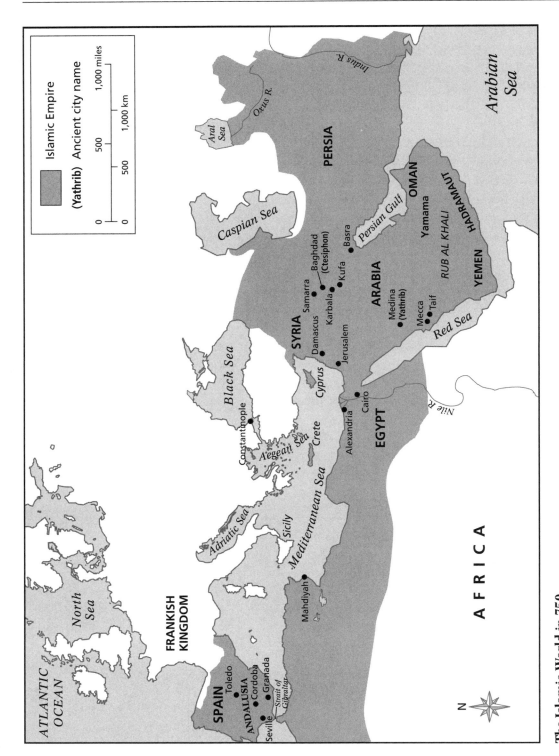

The Islamic World in 750
Under the reign of the Umayyad caliphs, the Islamic Empire expanded across Europe, Africa, and Asia, reaching its largest size. The end of the dynasty in 750 also marked the end of Islamic conquests.

opposition group was led by Abd Allah ibn az-Zubayr (d. 692), the son of one of Muhammad's companions. Abd Allah took control of Mecca and proclaimed himself caliph; he attracted many followers–and prolonged the Second Civil War.

The war dragged on for 12 years. Soldiers, supplies, and weapons were used to wage this internal conflict, rather than to expand the empire. By 692, Abd al-Malik had taken firm control of the Islamic Empire, squelching any opposition. After recapturing Mecca, Abd al-Malik's forces killed Abd Allah, sending his head to the caliph in Damascus. Until 750, a succession of Umayyad caliphs would rule the empire.

With the civil war finally at an end, the Muslims turned again to conquering new lands. This second phase of conquest served a number of important purposes. First, it enabled the empire to grow and expand. Soldiers eagerly signed on for the new conquests, hoping for wealth or a place in heaven. Second, the battles with enemies outside the empire turned the focus of the Muslims away from the problems at home. Third, the conquests were the perfect avenue for spreading Islam.

The new conquests were extensive. More of Africa fell, enabling the Muslims to advance to the coast of Morocco. From here, an army made up largely of Berbers began a push into Spain in 711. The troops were led by general Tariq ibn Ziyad, who took control of the southeastern two-thirds of the Iberian Peninsula.

The Umayyad armies of conquest were very different from the raiding parties that had attacked Meccan caravans during the time of Muhammad. Separated by tribe into divisions, the armies were highly organized. Mirroring the way their enemies fought, the Muslims adapted to a closed formation, staying tightly together while fighting. Fourteenth-century Arab historian Ibn Khaldun (quoted in John Jandora's *Militarism in Arab Society*) explained why the early Umayyad armies favored the closed attack: "They sought to die in holy war because they wished to persevere and were firm in their faith. The advance in close order is more appropriate for seeking death." Bows and arrows, as well as swords, were still the weapons of choice.

One of the chief aims of the second wave of conquests was to capture Constantinople, the capital of the Byzantine Empire, which was Christian. Earlier caliphs had unsuccessfully tried to conquer the city. Now, under the caliph Sulayman, the Muslims tried again. From 716 to 717, Islamic troops laid siege to the city. The attacks were very costly– the Islamic fleet and army from Syria were wiped out–and in the end the

THE SHIITE MARTYR

Today, al-Husayn is remembered by Shiites as a martyr to their cause. His burial site in Karbala, in present-day southwestern Iraq, is considered a holy site by Shiites. Each year, on the first day of Muharram (the first month of the Islamic calendar), Shiite Muslims commemorate Husayn's martyrdom. The 10-day period of mourning includes penance, selfflagellation (beating), mourning processions, and a passion play about Husayn's death called the *taziya*.

The Berbers

The Berbers, nomadic people of North Africa, strongly resisted any efforts to convert them to Islam. When they finally did embrace Islam, however, they proved to be fierce fighters. Berber armies were instrumental in helping the Muslims conquer Spain. These Berber conquerors of Spain came to be known as the Moors. Later, the Berbers supported the kingdoms that sprang up in North Africa to rival the caliphate in Baghdad.

The term *Barbary Coast*, a section of North Africa's shoreline, was derived from the word Berber. Beginning in the 16th century, Berber and Arab pirates terrorized European trading ships that sailed along this stretch of ocean. Today, the Berbers are a significant part of the population in Morocco and Algeria.

attempts to take Constantinople were not successful. Throughout the history of the Islamic Empire, Constantinople remained outside of Islamic control (although it later fell to the Muslims under the Ottoman Empire during the 15th century).

From Spain, the Muslim armies pushed across the Pyrenees, a mountain range in Europe that separates Spain from France. In 732, the Muslim advance was stopped near the Loire River in southeastern France by Charles Martel (c. 688–741). Charles was the leader of the Franks, a people who lived in parts of modern Germany, France, and the Netherlands. This marked the farthest extent of the Islamic Empire in Europe.

Despite their failure on this front, the Muslims in 827 began raiding Sicily and southern Italy, as well as the Mediterranean coastal regions of France and Italy known as the Riviera. Here, the Muslims were more successful. They held Sicily until the middle of the 11th century.

In the East, the Muslim armies pushed from Iran into central Asia, to an area just south of the Aral Sea that is now Uzbekistan. They also moved into the Indus River Valley. Muhammad ibn al-Qasim, a 17-year-old general, took his troops from southern Iran to Daibul, the biggest city in the Indus delta. From here, they went to conquer cities in what is now Pakistan.

Despite the enlargement of the empire, opposition to the Umayyads continued to grow in the late eighth century. Many Muslims were opposed to economic changes instituted by the Umayyad caliphs, including tax breaks for non-Arab Muslims. The Umayyads also spent vast amounts of money building and furnishing opulent palaces. Preferential treatment for Umayyad relatives and friends continued to rankle many. Although later Umayyad caliphs tried to address the economic and social issues facing the empire, they generally were unsuccessful. By this time, most people were so dissatisfied with the Umayyads that they were ready for a bigger change.

The Shiites continued to stage uprisings against the Umayyad rulers. The most powerful opposition group, however, was the Abbasids in eastern Persia. The Abbasids were descendants of al-Abbas (d. 652), an uncle of Muhammad. They launched a massive propaganda campaign against the Umayyads. Using groups of people who despised the ruling caliph, they put out the word that the Umayyads were too royal and not pious enough. The Abbasids also spread the message that *they* were the true successors of Muhammad, not the Umayyads. The Abbasids managed to unite the various opposition groups against the ruling dynasty, asking for support for the true "family of Muhammad."

In 747, the Abbasids and other Umayyad enemies united under a black banner and rebelled against the Umayyads. The Abbasid revolution lasted three years. When the fighting was over, the Abbasids and their allies had put an end to the dynasty that had lasted fewer than 100 years and 14 caliphs.

The Abbasids were not quite finished with the Umayyads, however. After their victory, the new rulers invited 80 Umayyad leaders to a huge banquet. During this "feast of peace," hired assassins suddenly attacked the guests, bludgeoning them to death with clubs. The Abbasids threw leather covers over the dead and dying and continued eating their dinner. From this point on, the first Abbasid caliph would call himself *al-saffah*, which means "blood shedder."

One of the Umayyad princes managed to escape the massacre. Abd al-Rahman (r. 756–788) soon founded a dynasty in Spain that rivaled the Abbasids in glory and power (see page 44). In fact, after the fall of the Umayyad Dynasty, the cultural, religious, and economic interconnectedness of the Islamic Empire remained, but politically the empire was never totally unified.

The Abbasid Dynasty

The first Abbasid caliph was Abu al-Abbas al-Saffah (d. 754), the man who had masterminded the Abbasid revolution. His first few years as caliph were spent squelching any resistance or rivalry. Anyone who

CONNECTIONS >>>>>>>>>>>>>>

Geography in Spain

Muslim territory in Spain was known as al-Andalus. Today, the region is known as Andalusia, and a type of horse that originated in Spain is known as the Andalusian.

The Strait of Gibraltar, located between Africa and Spain, is named in honor of the Berber general Tariq ibn Ziyad. In 711, Tariq crossed the 13-mile-wide body of water, landing on the large rock that also bears his name: In Arabic, the rock is Jabal Tariq (Gibraltar), which means "mount of Tariq."

had helped the Abbasids gain power, and had therefore proven themselves willing to challenge the caliph, was killed to prevent them from stirring up any more trouble in the future. This included the Shiites, who had been so important to Abbasid victory during the revolution. By 756, new leaders were firmly in control of the Islamic Empire, and the Abbasid Dynasty ruled the empire for the next five centuries, until its demise in 1258.

Under the Abbasids, the capital of the empire moved from Damascus in modern Syria to Baghdad in modern Iraq. In 762, the second Abbasid caliph, Abu Jafa al-Mansur (d. 775), founded Baghdad. The new city signaled not just an end to the old Umayyad Dynasty, but a

Modern Baghdad
This photo of a food market in downtown Baghdad was taken in 1998. Through centuries of upheaval, Baghdad has remained a vibrant, beautiful city.

CONNECTIONS >>>>>>>>>>>>>>>>>

Watering the Desert

Under the Abbasids, the huge Islamic Empire needed to find ways to increase the production of food crops. Agriculture became a major concern. Islamic scientists translated and studied Greek and other ancient texts on farming, and they also added new knowledge to the field.

The demand for an increase in the variety and amount of new food crops led to a serious need for good irrigation and water management techniques. Islamic scholars and farmers rose to the occasion. Coming from a dry, desert climate, the Arabs early on understood the importance of making effective and efficient use of available water.

In Spain, the Umayyads introduced scientific methods of irrigation borrowed from the Egyptians, including water wheels, canals, reservoirs, and pumps. As agriculture flourished throughout the region, Spain quickly earned the reputation as the garden of Europe. Other scientific methods of farming introduced into Spain included the use of new fertilizers to help crops grow; knowledge about tree grafting and plant diseases; cross pollination of plants; and soil rehabilitation.

beginning of Abbasid power and glory. The city remained the empire's capital—as well as its political and cultural heart—for nearly 500 years.

The beginning of the Abbasid Dynasty also signaled an end to the age of Islamic conquest. The empire at the time stretched from Spain in the west to the borders of India in the east, from central Asia in the north to North Africa in the south. It entered a period of peace and prosperity, a "golden age" of Islamic civilization. Despite many advances in culture and learning, however, the Abbasids would soon lose control over their empire. A new age was coming, and it would not be long before the dynasty was reduced to nothing more than a puppet controlled by other powers within the empire.

CHAPTER 3

The Last Years of the Empire

LIKE THE UMAYYADS BEFORE THEM, THE ABBASIDS FACED THE hostility and resentment of the Shiites. Although the Shiites had helped the Abbasids take control of the empire, the Abbasids had proved less than grateful. Throughout the following years, the relationship between the Abbasids and the Shiites fluctuated between tolerance and persecution.

There was also fighting and conflict within the Abbasids' own family. Because they did not practice primogeniture (in which the oldest son inherits his father's land and title), the Abbasid caliphs could name anyone they wanted to succeed them. The result was that different family factions supported certain brothers, sons, or other male relatives for control of the empire and there was much infighting and little trust between relatives.

In 809, a bloody civil war erupted between two Abbasid half-brothers, Amin (d. 813) and Mamun (786–833). Although Amin had been chosen by his father, the caliph Harun al-Rashid, Mamun wanted control of the empire. Mamun killed Amin in 813, but the civil war continued for six more years.

As time went by, the bitter infighting—and the huge size of the empire itself—took a toll on the dynasty. Several areas split off from the caliphate, becoming autonomous states that effectively governed themselves. Spain and North Africa are two examples of regions that had their own dynasties or local governments.

As time wore on, even areas that were still nominally part of the Abbasid caliphate were actually ruled by local governors, tribes, or strong families. In 820, for example, a general named Tahir who had been appointed governor of Khurasan in Persia claimed control of the region.

Soon, other Persian governors were following his lead. Even though they claimed allegiance to the Abbasids, they functioned as separate states. By 836, things were so bad for the caliph in Baghdad that he moved the capital of his empire 60 miles up the Tigris River to Samarra.

By the 940s, the Abbasid caliphs were little more than figureheads. They held symbolic authority as religious leaders, but they had lost all control of the political, military, and governmental power of the empire. This state of affairs continued until the destruction of Baghdad in 1258. In 945, the first of the Abbasids' "protectors" began running the empire. Ahmad ibn Buyeh, a member of the powerful Buyid family from northwestern Iran, took control of Baghdad and was named commander-in-chief. The Buyids displaced the Turkish guards who had previously been in control.

The Buyids divided up the empire, granting various brothers and cousins control of different regions. Soon, the Buyids, like the Abbasids, were competing with one another to take full control of the Abbasids and their empire. While some regions were very well run and grew into thriving centers of commerce and culture, others were not.

The Buyids managed to remain the protectors of the Abbasids until 1055, when the Seljuk Turks took over what was left of the Islamic Empire. Under the Seljuks, Islamic conquest was taken up once again. The Seljuks eventually expanded into Byzantium, laying the foundation for the Ottoman Empire and, later, modern Turkey.

Like the Buyids before them, the Seljuks kept the Abbasids on as religious figureheads, allowing them to keep the title of caliph. The Seljuks themselves took the title of sultan, as well as king of the East and the West. Seljuk control of the empire marked the start of a strong Turkish influence and the decline of Arab influence.

Spain Splits Off

By the time the Seljuks took control of the empire, other areas had long ago separated themselves from Abbasid control. One of the first regions to split off from the caliphate was Spain. In 755, Abd al-Rahman, the Umayyad prince who had escaped being murdered when the Abbasids took control (see page 39), fled to North Africa. He eventually reached Spain and took over, setting up his own Umayyad state there.

At first, the rulers of this new dynasty called themselves *amirs*, or "commanders." This meant that they nominally accepted the Abbasid rulers as the caliphs of the empire. But in the late 920s, things changed.

Abd al-Rahman III (891–961) claimed for himself the title of caliph, or "commander of the faithful."

To celebrate his self-appointed title, Abd al-Rahman III established his capital at Madinat al-Zahra, three miles west of Cordoba. The magnificent city included a mosque, palace, government offices, markets, bathhouses, and beautiful gardens. The new caliph offered silver coins to anyone who would settle in his new city.

Madinat al-Zahra, built into the hillside, hammered home the social hierarchy. The caliph lived on the highest of three terraces; government officials lived and worked on the second terrace; soldiers and the rest of the citizens lived on the lowest level, near the markets and bath houses.

Under the Umayyads, Spain remained a center of Islamic culture until 1031. At that time, it was divided into a number of city-states. To prevent the Catholic kings in northern Spain from conquering Muslim areas, the city-states invited the Almoravids, Berber rulers from Morocco, to take control around 1085. For more than 100 years, Almoravid and Almohad (another group of Muslim Berbers) rulers controlled the area.

Watering the Palace
Part of the aqueduct that brought water to the Alhambra remains in Granada. The Muslims, who were accustomed to living in desert regions, celebrated the abundant water supply in Spain by adding many pools and fountains to their buildings.

Granada, the last Muslim stronghold in al-Andalus was finally taken in 1492 by the army of Catholic monarchs Ferdinand (1452–1516) and Isabella (1451–1504) of Spain. The Catholic monarchs immediately set about restoring Christianity to their land, giving Muslims the option to convert or return to North Africa. Any Muslim who chose to remain a Muslim and stay in Spain was hunted down and killed. In an effort to wipe out all traces of Islam in Granada, more than 1 million Arabic books were burned in the public square. By the early 1500s, the Inquisition, a special religious court that had begun in 1478 to forcibly convert Jews and root out heresy, had turned its attention to the Muslims. Any Muslims who had managed to escape the first waves of forced baptism or execution were now subjected to a second attack.

North Africa and the Fatimids

From the earliest days of the empire, the more distant areas of Africa were less subject to the control of the caliphate and the central government. Additionally, many Berbers were converted by the Kharijites, who were outside the mainstream of Sunni Islam and always opposed the reigning caliphs. As a result, separate Islamic states were set up in what are now Libya, Tunisia, and Algeria. Soon, the Kharijite groups had spread to modern-day Chad, Niger, and Mali.

The first rival African kingdom was established around 800. At this time, the Abbasid caliph was forced to recognize North African governor Ibrahim ibn al-Aghlab as hereditary governor. This meant the governorship could be passed on to his relatives. For the next 100 years, the Aghlabids ruled the area and paid only nominal homage to the Abbasids.

The most powerful rival kingdom in Africa was run by the Fatimids, a Shiite family originally from southwestern Persia. The Fatimids took control of North Africa in 909. The family was headed by Ubayd Allah (871–934), who claimed to be descended from Ali's wife Fatima, who was Muhammad's daughter. The Fatimids believed Ubayd Allah was the rightful caliph of the Islamic Empire. He also claimed to be the *mahdi*, the Rightful Leader, whose prophesied return is believed to usher in the end of the age.

After seizing North Africa with the help of Berber tribes, the Fatimids took the title of caliph. In 914, they founded a new capital called Mahdiyah (in what is now Tunisia). Although the Fatimids despised the Abbasids, they laid out their towns in much the same way as Baghdad, in a circular pattern with the palace at its center.

The Oud and the Guitar

The Arab musical instrument, the oud, led to the development of the lute in Spain. In fact, the word lute comes from the Arabic phrase *al oud*. The lute is a musical instrument with a pear-shaped body and six pairs of strings. The lute and other stringed instruments helped create a new class of performing artists in Europe: minstrels and troubadours. These skilled musicians moved from city to city strumming on ouds and other instruments, singing ballads, folk songs, and Christmas carols. Troubadours became very popular and well-respected in royal courts throughout Europe in the 12th and 13th centuries.

The guitar, which is a member of the lute family, may also have originated in Spain. The word *guitar*, which comes from the Arabic word *qitara*, originally was used to describe a flat-backed, four-stringed instrument. The guitar was easier to play than the lute, and by the late 1500s, it had surpassed its cousin in popularity in Spain and other parts of Europe. As the years went on, a fifth and then a sixth string were added to the guitar.

The guitar and Arabic music influenced the development of flamenco music in the Andalusia region of Spain. Flamenco combines guitar music with singing, dancing, and rhythmic clapping to create a unique and dramatic performance style. Historians believe that Flamenco combines Arabic, Roma (Gypsy), and Spanish musical styles from the medieval period. Today, flamenco is still a popular art form in Spain.

The oud is still a popular instrument in the Middle East, as this Kuwaiti ensemble illustrates.

The Fatimids were perhaps the most majestic of all the caliphs. Anything the caliph touched was considered sacred. His clothing or even the sight of him was considered to have *baraka*, or grace, which was passed on to anyone who saw him or came in contact with him. The caliph was also thought to be able to heal the sick and bring rain to dry areas.

Sicily

Sicily was the only other region in Europe that the Islamic Empire managed to conquer and control for a significant period of time. Aghlabids, Muslim Berbers from North Africa, first captured Sicily in 827. In 909, the Fatimids defeated the Aghlabids and took control of Sicily and North Africa. Under Islamic control, Palermo became a center of culture, knowledge, and commerce. It was famous for sugar, flax, olives, and silk weaving. By the 11th century, the island had about 300 mosques, according to contemporary Muslim reports.

When the Normans (people from Normandy, a region in what is today northwestern France) conquered the region after about 250 years of Muslim rule, they were impressed with the island's sophisticated culture. Unlike the Catholics in Spain, the Normans did not try to rid Sicily of all Muslim influences. The Norman ruler, Roger (c. 1031–1101), allowed Muslims to continue practicing their religion, welcomed Muslim soldiers into his army, and embraced Muslim scholars. Although he was a Christian, Roger's love of Islamic culture earned him the name "the Pagan." On his coronation day, the new king of Sicily wore a coronation robe with Arabic words stitched into it. He also continued to follow the Islamic calendar.

The Muslim cultural influence in Sicily continued for centuries. Frederick II of Sicily (1272–1337), who later became Holy Roman Emperor, dressed in Muslim fashions and kept a harem (a group of women, usually relatives including multiple wives, who lived in a secluded part of the house). Arab scholars and administrators were a key part of his court, and Arabic was one of the four official Sicilian languages. It was at Frederick's University of Naples that St. Thomas Aquinas was first exposed to Arabic translations of classical Greek texts.

The Fatimids faced internal opposition, but managed to hold onto power in North Africa for two centuries. One of their major accomplishments was seizing control of Egypt in 969. The loss of Egypt, a lucrative, money-making province, was a serious blow to the Abbasids. The Fatimids established Cairo—now the capital of Egypt—and founded Al-Azhar University, which is the oldest continuously open university in the world.

From 975 to 1036, the Fatimid caliphs were the most powerful in the Islamic Empire. (At one point the Friday prayers in Mecca and Medina were actually changed, offering blessings to the Fatimid caliph in Egypt instead of the Abbasid caliph in Baghdad.) Although they got much support in many areas of the kingdom, the Fatimids were not recognized in Baghdad, the acknowledged Islamic capital. They eventually weakened and, in the 11th century, were defeated by the Seljuk Turks, who were now the "protectors" of the Abbasid dynasty.

By 1073, the once-powerful Fatimids were in the same position as their Abbasid enemies: reduced to puppets under the control of powerful viziers and military commanders. In 1171, Kurdish military leader Salah al-Din (1138–1193), known in the West as Saladin, seized control of Egypt and brought an end to the Fatimid Dynasty. Salah al-Din's descendants controlled Egypt until 1250, when Turkish slave soldiers called the Mamluks took control. The Mamluks were the last great dynasty of the Islamic Empire.

Challenges from Without

The challenges the ruling Abbasids faced from within their own empire made it easier for those outside of the empire to begin attacking and chipping away at Muslim territories. The first outside challenge to Islamic power came in the early 11th century from the Turkmen, tribes of semi-nomadic Turkish-speaking people. Around that time, famine caused the Turkmen to begin migrating into northern Iran. As they moved into Muslim-held areas, the Turkmen defeated area tribes, taking control of the region. Eventually one group, the Seljuk Turks, became powerful enough to become the Abbasid caliphs' new "protectors." Under the Seljuk Turks, the Turkmen advanced into other areas that were controlled by the Byzantine Empire. The Turks brought Islam to these areas.

The Crusades

In 1095, Pope Urban II (c. 1042–1099) called on all good Christians to retake the Holy Land, particularly the city of Jerusalem, from the

Crusaders Victorious
This 14th-century French illuminated manuscript shows a scene from the First Crusade. The story is told from a European point of view.

"heathen" Muslims. More than 30,000 Europeans responded, and set out for the Middle East on the First Crusade. On the way to Jerusalem, the Crusaders captured the Muslim regions of what are now Syria, Lebanon, and Israel. They established a number of "crusader kingdoms," small states controlled by the Christian conquerors.

The most important crusader kingdom was the Latin Kingdom of Jerusalem, which the Christians captured in 1099. Upon entering the city, the Christian soldiers showed themselves to be far less merciful than the conquering Muslims had been. Crusaders slaughtered the Muslims and Jews of the city, and even Eastern Christians, considered to be heretics by the Roman Catholic Church.

Christian control of the Holy Land did not last long. In 1188, Salah al-Din took back Jerusalem, and over the coming years took control of the other crusader kingdoms. The Crusades had more significance for Europe than they did for the people of the Islamic Empire. For the people of Islam, the crusades were merely routine conflicts for control of various regions. In fact, most people of the Islamic Empire looked upon the crusaders as invading barbarians from a civilization much cruder and less advanced than their own.

One unanticipated byproduct of the Crusades was to facilitate the spread of Islamic goods, culture, and thought to Europe. Not only did the Crusaders learn Islamic military techniques (including the use of pigeons to carry messages), but they also brought home goods that soon became very popular, including spices, foods, and textiles. More luxurious goods brought from the East included rugs, glass mirrors, cosmetics, dyes, and soap.

The Mongols

The challengers who would ultimately bring an end to the Islamic Empire came not from Europe but from central Asia. In the early 1200s, a Mongol leader named Genghis Khan (c. 1167–1227) and his family conquered most of China, Russia, Iran, Anatolia, and Iraq. Genghis Khan began his raids into Islamic territory in 1219. He established himself in what is now Uzbekistan and worked his way south into northern Persia. In 1256, Genghis Khan's grandson, Hulagu (1217–1265), continued further through Persia, destroying Assassin groups along the way and moving into Iraq.

The Mongol conquests were extremely destructive. Cities and their residents were wiped out and irrigation projects destroyed, which ruined the farming of the region.

In 1258, Hulagu entered Baghdad itself. Here, the Mongol soldiers massacred thousands of people and the caliph's palace was

CONNECTIONS >>>>>>>>>>>>

Rosary Beads

Rosary beads, strings of beads used by Roman Catholics to count prayers, were borrowed by the Spanish St. Dominic (c. 1170–1221) from an Islamic practice. Muslims use a chain of 99 beads to count off the 99 different names of God.

The Origin of Assassins

The Assassins were a secret organization, a radical branch of the Sevener Shiites. The group was started around 1090 by a Persian who claimed to be descended from tribal kings in Southern Arabia. The Assassins had their headquarters in the mountains of northern Iran. From here, the group raided and took control of other fortresses. The Assassins also became known for their bloody methods of getting rid of those who stood in their way. Targets were often prominent Sunni political or religious leaders. The Assassin's favorite method of killing was the dagger.

The term *assassin* comes from the Arabic word *hashshash*, which, translated literally, means a person who uses hashish—a mind-altering drug. Legend has it that some of the lower members of the group, the ones who performed the actual killings, were controlled by other members through the use of hashish. However, *hashshash* can also mean a useless person. Today, an assassin is defined as a person who murders a politically prominent person.

destroyed. The caliph, his family, and his officials were also killed to make sure no one remained to claim control. By 1260, most of the Islamic east was under Mongol control and the Islamic Empire was no more.

Muslim influence continued, however, under the Ottoman Turks, who founded an empire that lasted until the 20th century (see page 115).

PART II

SOCIETY AND CULTURE

Society in the Islamic Empire

Living in the Islamic Empire

Islamic Art, Science, and Culture

CHAPTER 4

Society in the Islamic Empire

AS THE ISLAMIC EMPIRE GREW AND EXPANDED, ITS GOVERN-
ment had to evolve to meet the needs of the changing situation. The different styles of government and leadership throughout the history of the
empire reflect the efforts of caliphs to maintain control of the wide variety of lands and people in their realms.

The Caliphate and the Umayyad Dynasty

The first governmental organization of the Islamic Empire centered on the
caliph, the successor of Muhammad. The caliph was both the spiritual
and political leader of the empire. The caliph's authority as the supreme
leader of the Umma was unquestioned.

The caliphate was an Islamic theocracy, a government in which religious rulers govern in the name of God. There was no separation of religion and government. The laws of the empire were based upon the
Quran and the example set by Muhammad.

Sunni Muslims believed that the first four rightly guided caliphs set
the example for all caliphs. They were all Arabs from Muhammad's tribe
and most of them were chosen by a council of leaders who represented the
entire Umma. After the first four caliphs, however, this example was rarely
followed. That is why although the Umayyad leaders continued to call
themselves caliphs, some experts consider the Umayyad Dynasty less a
caliphate than a kingdom.

Muawiya, the first Umayyad caliph, moved his dynasty toward a
monarchy by establishing a line of succession and elevating the caliph
and his courtiers to a higher class in the empire's social structure. Although the first caliphs made themselves accessible to ordinary citizens,

OPPOSITE
Behind the Veil
*Islamic law requires women
to dress modestly, but this
has meant different things at
different times. In some
Islamic countries today,
women may not show more
than their eyes in public.*

Muawiya began to act in a more royal manner. He appointed a door-keeper to decide who could or could not see the caliph. The first Umayyad caliph also created a royal bodyguard, made up of soldiers, who accompanied him everywhere he went. Later Umayyad caliphs relied even more heavily on the military to help them wield power.

The Umayyads were the first caliphs who had to deal with a newly expanded empire, and under them the Islamic Empire grew to its largest size. At a time when travel and communication over large distances was slow and difficult, the caliph could not personally keep firm control over all of his holdings. To make sure things continued to run smoothly in the conquered lands, the local system of government was usually left in place. Then, to ensure cooperation, the caliph divided the empire into regions and appointed strong, capable governors to oversee them.

Governorships were, at first, awarded to the caliph's relatives or other upper class Arabs. Later, they were given to army commanders and other leaders who had demonstrated some ability. In some cases, governors were appointed for life or were allowed to pass on their position to their relatives. In most cases, however, the caliph chose to rotate the governors. In some regions, for example, the governors were replaced almost yearly. This kept them under control and ensured that they would not become too powerful.

The governor's duties were many and varied. Of course, he had to continue to acknowledge the caliph as the supreme leader of the empire. The governor also had to raise an army and be prepared to send his troops to defend the empire whenever necessary.

But the governor's most important job was to collect taxes from the citizens of his territory. These taxes were the lifeblood of the Islamic Empire. As long as revenues from the territories continued to fill the caliphate's treasury, the governor was allowed a large measure of autonomy and control in his area.

At home, the Umayyads worked to centralize government functions. They moved the heart of the new empire to Syria (Syria was the first region outside of Arabia conquered by the Muslims). From here, the caliph was able to administer and control his many provinces. In addition, the Umayyads instituted a number of bureaucratic innovations. For example, they set up the first postal service. Riders on horseback delivered messages from one part of the empire to another. The Umayyads also established a bureau of registry and were the first Islamic rulers to mint coins in silver and gold.

The Royal Abbasid Dynasty

Although the Umayyads set the precedent for the caliph as king, the Abbasids took the concept to a whole new level. The new dynasty followed the lead of Persian royalty, assigning themselves divine powers and demanding total authority in all matters, both religious and political.

The Abbasid caliphs and their families also wrapped themselves in a mantle of mystery and ceremony, taking the idea of royalty to new heights. In *The Arabs in History*, Bernard Lewis says the "new dignity of the Caliph was expressed in new titles, and in a much more elaborate ceremonial." Unlike the earliest caliphs, the Abbasid rulers held themselves and their family apart from the common people. Instead of going through a doorkeeper, as in Umayyad times, people hoping to meet with the Abbasid caliphs had to first make their pleas to a series of chamberlains. Rulers rarely appeared in public, but when they did, they wore expensive silk robes and were doused in rare perfumes. Those who did see the caliph had to follow an elaborate routine that included kissing the ground and avoiding eye contact with the ruler.

Under the Abbasids, the government of the empire became even more efficient than it had been under the Umayyads. The early Abbasid caliphs created a centralized system of administration, whose main function was to efficiently collect, control, and spend revenues that were raised through taxation (see the box on 58).

The bureaucracy associated with the Abbasid government was huge. By the middle of the ninth century, the Abbasids' administration was made up of several departments called *diwans*. They included the treasury, the accounting department, the intelligence department, a chancery department that handled all official correspondence, and a court of appeals. Every aspect of government was handled through the diwans and the thousands of clerks and secretaries who worked in them.

Capital City
This Persian miniature painting (date unknown) shows the Abbasid capital, Baghdad.

Taxes and the Abbasid Dynasty

The huge army and bureaucratic structure of the Abbasid caliphate required a constant and steady flow of funds. These funds were collected by taxing those who lived throughout the empire. The two main taxes were the land tax and the head tax.

The land tax, called the *kharaj*, was levied on all landowners throughout the empire, whether Muslim or non-Muslim. The goods produced on a landowner's property—grain, fruit, and livestock—were also subject to taxation. The rate of taxation for Arab Muslims was lower than the rate paid by other Muslims and non-Muslims. Some Arab Muslims were exempted from paying the tax at all.

The head tax, or *jizya*, was levied on all Jews and Christians. The taxation rate depended upon the wealth of the taxpayer. Other taxes included those on imported and exported merchandise and crafts made in the cities.

Under the Abbasids, the importance and power of high-born Arab officials and army officers declined. Government offices and positions of authority were now awarded to those who were most capable, not those of a certain ancestry. In the earliest days of the Abbasid Dynasty, the people who had run the government before the Islamic conquest continued to do the same work after the Muslims took over. In Baghdad, this meant a highly educated class of Persian officials. During the Abbasid caliphate, these Persian secretaries enjoyed great wealth and influence. The caliph and his assistants also selected freed slaves and members of the ruler's household whom they believed were best-suited for high-ranking government positions. As a result, many Christians, Jews, and Zoroastrians were involved in the workings of the Islamic government.

The Abbasid Dynasty marked the rise of *wazirs*, or viziers. Viziers were top-level administrators—professional, highly educated men who were knowledgeable in literature, writing, management, taxation, and many other areas. The Abbasid caliphs came to depend heavily upon their viziers, especially in later years when the caliph became less involved in government and more involved in leading a life of pleasure. The viziers, many of whom were Persian, consequently became extremely powerful. During the later years of the dynasty, many viziers effectively ran the empire while the caliph served merely as a figurehead and religious symbol.

One of the most powerful families of viziers was the Barmecides, who served the first five Abbasid caliphs. The Barmecides were Persians who had converted to Islam. The Barmecide viziers were much-beloved by the people of Baghdad, who considered them to be capable, intelligent, and generous. In the early 800s, it seemed that the Barmecide viziers had it all. The vizier Jafar served under caliph Harun al-Rashid (766-809). As a token of his esteem for Jafar, the caliph allowed the vizier to marry his favorite sister, Abbasah. However, the match was meant to be an honorary one only. When Abbasah became pregnant, the end was near for the Barmecides. Jafar was eventually executed by his former supporter. The caliph Rashid also had a number of Jafar's family members imprisoned and confiscated their property and wealth.

As time went on, the huge Abbasid bureaucracy became too expensive to support. As more people around the empire converted to Islam, the amount of tax revenue decreased. Financial problems led the Abbasid caliphs to require governors to pay for and maintain regional armies and bureaucracies. This strengthened the role of the governor while weakening that of the caliph. As time went on, the governors were effectively running—and ruling—their provinces.

By the 940s, the Abbasids in Baghdad were reduced to mere symbols, with other groups, known as "protectors," controlling the empire. These protectors were often army commanders who had taken advantage of the weakening caliphate to seize control. Although the government structure remained the same, the caliph was now the leader of the empire and the Islamic faith in name only. One such group of protectors was the Seljuk Turks. After they took control of the empire in 1050, they gave themselves the title of *sultan*.

The Military

Under the first four caliphs, the army was made up of Arabs, Bedouins, and others who had volunteered to spread the word of Islam and conquer other nations. Although the early army was loosely organized, it was an important and effective fighting force in the Islamic Empire. Being a soldier for the empire was quickly recognized as a sure way to gain land and booty. Those who took part in conquests were awarded pensions and did not have to pay the land tax required of all other landowners in the empire.

Under the Umayyads, the makeup of the army changed to include many Syrians. Under the Abbasids, many Persians entered the army's ranks. The army itself also became leaner and more organized. Instead of being made up of Arab volunteers from various tribes, the army was soon made up of trained units of non-Arab professional soldiers. Volunteers were still accepted, but only when they were needed.

HARUN AL-RASHID AND CHARLEMAGNE

During the early ninth century, the two most powerful rulers in the world were Caliph Harun al-Rashid in the East and Charlemagne (742-814) in the West. Charlemagne, leader of the Franks, was the grandson of Charles Martel, who had turned back the Muslim advance into France in 732. The two struck up a relationship, sending gifts to one another. Among the gifts sent to Charlemagne by the Abbasid caliph were fabrics, perfumes, and exotic animals, including an elephant.

This trend toward hiring professionals started in 833, when the Caliph al-Mutasim (d. 842) decided to create an army that was entirely loyal to him, with few ties to others in the community. Before, the army had been made up of separate groups commanded by strong leaders. Troops were often more loyal to their leaders than to the caliph himself. To create an army of loyal troops, Mutasim recruited mostly Turks, slaves, and freed slaves. Many of the caliph's new troops did not even speak Arabic. To ensure that his loyal troops did not mingle or become involved with Baghdad's residents, Mutasim built a new capital, Samarra, 60 miles north of Baghdad.

The Turkish professional soldiers eventually came to dominate the army—and the caliphate. By 861, Turkish officers were able to place a caliph on the throne (al-Muntasir—they later assassinated him). By the 940s, the army's commander-in-chief was totally in control of the empire, calling himself the caliph's "protector."

Social Classes

The Islamic Empire, like other great civilizations before and after it, had specific social classes. Despite the Quran's admonition of equality, these classes existed throughout the empire. Only as non-Arabs intermarried with Arabs and family bloodlines became less distinct did the separations between some of the classes begin to blur.

Even before the advent of Islam, the Quraysh tribe in Mecca had represented a sort of Arab aristocracy. After the Umayyad and Abbasid caliphs took control, the most elite of the upper class were made up of the rulers, their families, and their officials and courtiers. Under the Umayyads, those officials and courtiers were often members of the Quraysh tribe to which the Umayyads belonged, as well as leaders of other Arab tribes. Under the Abbasids, Persian officials and courtiers were also selected for prestigious positions within the caliphate.

As the empire expanded, another upper-level social layer appeared. This class of people was made up of the Arab descendants of Muhammad's companions, as well as the descendants of those Arabs who had taken part in the wars of conquest. As early adherents of Islam, these people received pensions, large pieces of land, and special privileges.

Below the upper class of Arab Muslims were the *mawali*, an Arabic word that means "clients." The mawali were new Muslims, non-Arabs who converted to Islam after being conquered. To become a *mawla* (singular of mawali), non-Arabs had to be accepted by an Arab patron.

The mawali were not, at first, considered the equals of Arab Muslims. Although the Quran says they should have been treated the same way, this was not always the case. During the Umayyad period, for example, mawali were still taxed at a higher rate than Arab Muslims. Mawali in the army received lower pay than Arabs and usually had to fight as foot soldiers. Socially, marriages between mawali and Arabs were discouraged.

Over time, the mawali population in garrison towns actually outnumbered the Arabs there. As their numbers increased, the converts began to realize the enormous power and political leverage they might wield within the empire. Because of their dislike of Umayyad economic policies, many mawali joined the Shiites. As a result, the Shiite movement was strongest in Iraq, where Persian mawali lived. It quickly became clear to the Umayyad rulers that they must find a way to appease this growing class of people, and economic and social reforms were the result. After Umar II became caliph in 717, for example, he changed the tax structure to exempt the mawali from paying the same taxes non-Muslims paid.

A third class of people in the Islamic Empire were the *dhimmis*—people who followed religions that were protected under Islam. Dhimmis (the word means "protected minority") included Christians and Jews, whom Muslims considered "Peoples of the Book" because they followed the word of God as revealed by prophets in the Old and New Testaments of the Judeo-Christian Bible (Muslims recognize prophets who came before Muhammad, including Adam, Noah, Abraham, Moses, and Jesus).

In most parts of the empire, dhimmis were treated well. They often held important positions in government and owned and operated their own businesses. They were allowed to continue practicing their religion—in private.

Other Religions
This brass menorah from Morocco, a special lamp used during the Jewish holiday of Hanukkah, shows the influence of the Islamic Empire in the art motifs used to decorate it. Christians, Jews, and Zoroastrians were allowed to practice their religions, although with some restrictions.

Dhimmis throughout the empire were, however, under some restrictions. In addition to the land tax, which all members of the empire paid, they had to pay an additional head tax—a tax paid per person each year. In some parts of the empire, dhimmi had to carry certificates showing that they had indeed paid their yearly tax.

They were forbidden to build new houses of worship and could not try to convert others to their religion. They could not worship outside their church or synagogue. They could not ride horses or bear arms. They also had to wear distinctive clothing that signified their religion. They were not allowed to testify against a Muslim in a court of law, and they could not live in Mecca or Medina. Depending upon the current caliph, these and other restrictions might be eased or tightened.

Although the restrictions might seem designed to encourage dhimmis to convert to Islam, most Muslims were content to allow them to retain their own religions; the Muslims preferred having the income from the dhimmis' head tax.

The lowest class in Islamic society were slaves. Slavery was not a new practice; it had existed on the Arabian Peninsula long before Muhammad was born. In his teachings, Muhammad did not ban slavery. However, restrictions were placed on who could be enslaved and how slaves must be treated. As a result, Muhammad's teachings did improve the lot of enslaved people throughout the empire.

In the Quran, Muslims are forbidden to enslave other Muslims. They are also required to treat their slaves humanely. This included allowing slaves to marry or buy their own freedom. In addition, the Quran states that freeing one's slaves is pleasing to God and can absolve many sins.

Muslim armies enslaved people from all the regions they conquered. Men, women, and children from Africa, Turkey, Spain, and other areas were all enslaved to work for the Islamic Empire. Slaves could be bought at any large city's slave market. The trade itself was a lucrative one throughout the empire.

There were two different types of slaves: Those who worked in the home and those who served in the Islamic armies. In the eighth century, young men of Turkish origin were brought as slaves to major cities such as Baghdad to serve as palace guards. The caliphs also used enslaved Turkish soldiers as personal bodyguards.

Sometimes, slaves refused to passively accept their fate. In 869, an uprising of African slaves known as the Zanj resulted in the slaves seizing control of Basra and other areas in southern Iraq. They turned the tables on their former masters, taking Muslims as slaves to serve them. The Zanj were able to hold onto these areas until 883.

Despite their low social standing, some slaves played an important role in the history of the empire. Through the years, the most trusted and competent served not just as servants and soldiers but also as high-ranking government officials, advisors, temporary rulers, and concubines (women who were supported by men and lived with them without being legally married to them). Concubines who had children by their masters could not be sold or given away, and were freed when their masters died. The children of these relationships were free from birth.

One of the strongest indicators of the blurred lines between social classes occurred in the middle of the eighth century. In 744, Umayyad Caliph Yazid III ascended the throne. Yazid's mother, a captured Persian princess, was the slave and concubine of an earlier caliph. The last two Umayyad caliphs were also sons of slaves. And in later years slaves actually founded dynasties. The most famous of these is the Mamluk Dynasty.

CONNECTIONS >>>>>>>>>>>>

Slavic Slaves

In his book *A Middle East Mosaic*, author Bernard Lewis says that some of the most highly prized slaves in the Islamic Empire were Eastern Europeans, especially Slavs. This is the origin of the English word "slave."

Islamic Law

Islamic law, both moral and legal, is known as *sharia*, which may be translated as "the clear path that leads to God." All of the early laws throughout the empire were taken directly from the Quran and the Sunna. (Sunna is the example set by Muhammad through all of his words and deeds. These words and deeds were set down in collections of writings, known as Hadith, many years after Muhammad died.)

In the early days of the empire, most situations were easily covered by the Quran and the Hadith. If a question arose about how a problem or conflict should be handled, the caliph and religious scholars resolved the issue by interpreting various passages in these two sources. But as the empire expanded, Muslims came into contact with people whose cultures and customs were very different from their own. As new and unusual situations arose from this clash of cultures, situations arose that were not covered in the two holy sources. What could be done?

To solve new moral and legal dilemmas, the Muslims developed a branch of legal study that is known as *fiqh*. Fiqh involves reading and analyzing the divinely revealed sources of law, as well as applying human reason to situations not explicitly covered in the Quran and the Hadith. Those who study fiqh are called *fuqaha* (the singular is *faqih*).

To aid them in correctly interpreting the law, fuqaha looked to *ijma*, which means the consensus of the community. Ijma includes the rulings and actual practices of the faithful. In other words, ijma is the interpretation most commonly agreed upon by the majority of religious and legal scholars—a kind of legal precedent.

Another method of determining what is and is not lawful is *qiyas*, or reasoning based on analogy. This practice, followed by more liberal Sunni schools of law, involves comparing new situations to similar ones in the past, and drawing conclusions from the comparison.

Toward the end of ninth century, a number of schools of law, called madhhabs, developed throughout the empire. Some schools favored a stricter, more traditional way of interpreting law, using the Quran and the Hadith almost exclusively. Others favored a more liberal approach, particularly when the legal issues concerned non-religious aspects of life.

Four Sunni legal schools still exist.

1. The Hanafi school, founded in southern Iraq by religious scholar Abu Hanifa (699-767), followed a more liberal tradition of using qiyas. In the

CONNECTIONS >>>>>>>>>>>>>>>>

Sharia Today

In some countries where Islam dominates (or where there is a sizable Muslim minority), sharia is a code of conduct that is applied to the Muslim community. Nations where this is true include India, Egypt, Syria, Iraq, and Turkey.

In other countries, sharia is the law of the land. This is the case in Iran, Saudi Arabia, parts of Pakistan and Indonesia, and the northern part of Nigeria. In these countries, it is a crime to drink alcohol and for women to appear in public dressed "immodestly" (what constitutes "modesty" varies from country to country).

16th century, the Hanafi school was officially adopted by the Ottoman Turks. Today, it has the largest following of all the Sunni legal schools, and is followed in Turkey, India, and Pakistan.

2. The Hanbali school was founded in Baghdad by Ahmad ibn Hanbal (780-855). A more traditional school of law, Hanbali today is prevalent on the Arabian Peninsula.

3. The Shafii school, founded by Muhammad ibn Idris al-Shafii (767-820), tried to find a middle ground between the more traditional and the more liberal interpretations of the law. This school is now followed in Southeast Asia, parts of Egypt, and parts of the Arabian Peninsula.

Islamic Law and Personal Conduct

Islamic law recognizes five different categories of conduct for all human acts. These categories are:

• Required or obligatory

• Recommended

• Neutral or permissible

• Reprehensible or disapproved

• Forbidden

The Five Pillars of Islam (see page 18) are all required practices. Forbidden acts, also called haram, include eating pork, gambling, and practicing adultery.

4. The Maliki school, founded by Malik ibn Anas (716-795), followed a more traditional method of interpreting moral and legal law, and was supported by scholars in Mecca and Medina. Today, the Maliki school is followed in North Africa.

The Shiites and Kharijites follow their own schools of law, which have distinct differences from those of the Sunni Muslims. For example, Shiite law does not allow analogy in the interpretation of law. Instead, Shiite schools allow reasoning to determine law. Shiites follow two different schools of law. Mujtahidi is the dominant one in Iran.

CHAPTER 5

Living in the Islamic Empire

FROM THE EARLIEST DAYS OF CONQUEST, THE CALIPHS wanted to discourage Muslims from interacting with the conquered people. Under Umar, the second rightly guided caliph, the Muslims began the practice of building garrison towns in conquered regions, where the conquerors would live apart from the conquered. These garrison towns served several functions: they prevented problems from arising between Muslim troops and the newest subjects of the Islamic Empire; they kept Muslim troops from picking up the habits and customs of the newly conquered; and they made it possible for life in conquered cities and towns to continue functioning as normal.

Kufa

The first garrison town was Kufa, built by Umar's famous General Saad (see page 28) in southern Iraq in 638. Saad chose the site for its excellent grazing lands. Here, the soldiers' camels, horses, and sheep would be well fed. The town was built out of baked bricks and marble columns that were taken from nearby ruins, with Saad's home and the mosque in the center. Saad himself served as Kufa's governor.

In Kufa, the soldiers lived in areas of the city that were segregated by tribal affiliations; within a tribal district, one clan might all live on one specific street. As the garrison city grew, each tribal district built its own mosques and created its own associations.

As wives and children joined the soldiers, Kufa's population skyrocketed. Just a few years after its founding, it was home to more than 40,000 people. To support this growing population, merchants soon flocked to Kufa, building out from the center of the town.

OPPOSITE
Open-Air Supermarket
Spices, dried fruits, and beans are available at this open-air market in Baghdad. In the hot, dry climate of the Middle East, open markets known as bazaars have existed for thousands of years.

Over the years, Kufa developed into one of the most important cities in the empire. It became a Shiite political center, as well as a center for learning.

Basra

Another early garrison town in southern Iraq was Basra, founded by Umar in 635. In 665, the caliph Muawiya appointed his half-brother Ziyad commander of Basra. Ziyad was a strict disciplinarian and ruled the town with an iron fist. He was also a brilliant administrator, implementing an official registry department in Basra for official documents. Under Ziyad's command, all official documents were sealed with wax, then marked with the governor's own peacock stamp. Ziyad even persuaded Muawiya to follow his example, marking the first formalization of government documents in the Islamic Empire.

Baghdad

Baghdad, the most glorious city built by the Muslims during the Islamic Empire, was not founded as a garrison town. In 762, the Abbasid caliph Mansur decided he needed a new capital for himself and his descendants. Mansur wanted the new city in Iraq to serve as a symbol of the Abbasids' political, commercial, and cultural superiority. The new capital was erected on the site of an ancient Persian village that had also been named Baghdad. Although Mansur called his capital Madinat al-Salam, which means "City of Peace," people continued to call it by its old name.

Baghdad was located on the west bank of the Tigris River, 20 miles northeast of the former Persian capital, Ctesiphon. The site was wisely chosen. Located between the Tigris and the Euphrates Rivers, Baghdad was surrounded by fertile land. Additionally, the city could easily be defended from hostile forces: Enemy troops could attack only by ship or by crossing a heavily-guarded bridge into the city.

The most skilled builders and designers from around the empire were brought to Baghdad to work on the royal complex. About 100,000 workers toiled for four years to complete the Abbasid masterpiece. Known as the Round City, Baghdad originally was built in a circular plan and measured nearly 2 miles across. The city was made up of three concentric circles, each one surrounded by a wall. The caliph's palace and the mosque were built in the innermost circle. In the middle circle lived courtiers, army officers, and other important people. The third circle was occupied by the rest of the people.

THE DAMASCUS EXCEPTION

Not all of the caliphs believed in separating Muslims from the conquered. After taking control of Damascus, Muawiya did not set up a garrison town. Instead, Arabs mixed with the native Syrians, encouraging assimilation and cooperation. Muawiya himself married the daughter of a Syrian tribal leader.

The outermost wall was a strong one, with four different gates leading to the four different points of the empire. Each gate was defended by a company of 1,000 soldiers. Merchants and businessmen set up shop outside the outermost wall.

The city continued to grow and spread. By the early 800s, Baghdad was the largest city in the Middle East. At its height, more than 1 million people made their homes there. During the reign of the caliph Harun al-Rashid (r. 786–809), Baghdad expanded to the east side of the Tigris, and this area soon became the heart of the city.

In its heyday, the city was the most cultured, beautiful, and busy metropolitan area in the world. It contained breathtaking mosques, palaces, and gardens. Like other cities throughout the empire, Baghdad was home to libraries, colleges, and hospitals. The bustling Tigris served as an avenue of trade and a means of entertainment. Gondolas plied the water, filled with goods and people.

Located in the heart of the former Sassanian Empire, Baghdad's residents and visitors could not help but be influenced by Persian culture. As a result, a Persian influence began to spread throughout the empire. Eventually, only the Islamic religion and the Arabic language remained from the old Arab empire.

In addition to the Persian influence, the city enjoyed a truly international atmosphere. As capital of the far-flung Islamic Empire, Baghdad attracted people from all over the world to study and do business. Scholars, poets, scientists, and other learned people came to visit and study at the libraries, mosques, and schools. Harun al-Rashid himself had a library with close to 600,000 books.

Baghdad continued to be one of the most cultured and beautiful cities in the world until 1258, when it was sacked and destroyed by the Mongols. The destruction marked the end of the Islamic Empire.

Cairo

Another center of Islamic culture was Cairo in Egypt. Cairo, located

CONNECTIONS >>>>>>>>>>>>

Tennis, Anyone?

Although most people believe that tennis originated in the late 1200s in France, some historians believe the game's roots can be traced back to the Islamic Empire. The word *racket* comes from the Arabic word *rahat*, meaning the palm of the hand. The term may have been used for handball games. These games might have evolved into games where the ball was hit with a broad piece of wood. In fact, some historians believe the word *tennis* actually comes from the city of Tinnis in Egypt, where linen might have been used to make tennis balls.

CONNECTIONS >>>>>>>>>>>>

"Moorish" Architecture

The influence of the Islamic conquerors on architectural styles can still be seen today in areas that were once part of the Islamic Empire, especially in southern Spain. "Moorish" architecture made its way to the Americas with the earliest Spanish explorers. These explorers built houses, missions, and other buildings that reminded them of their homes back in Spain.

In the United States, the influence of Islamic architecture is especially strong in the Southwest. Here, Moorish touches can be seen in buildings that were built hundreds of years ago, as well as those built more recently. These touches include horseshoe-shaped archways, red-tiled roofs, smooth stucco outer walls, ceramic tiles, heavy wooden doors, and courtyards with a central fountain surrounded by arcades. The so-called Mediterranean Revival style of building, popular in Florida in the early 1900s, includes elements of Moorish, Spanish, Italian, Venetian, and other styles. Today, home builders can choose a "Spanish eclectic" type of home that incorporates some Moorish features into its design.

on the banks of the Nile River, was founded in 969 by the Fatimid Dynasty. It served as a center of government, culture, and commerce throughout the Fatimid period.

From Cairo, the Fatimids took control of the gold mines of Nubia, along the upper Nile. With Nubian gold, the Fatimids controlled one of the richest regions in the empire, enabling them to pay huge armies, buy supplies, and send out missionaries to convert people to Islam.

The Nile River was the center of life in Cairo and was treated with reverence and care. Maintaining the waterways and irrigation canals that watered the area's crops was an important part of the caliph's duties. The Nile also served as the means for transporting goods, people, and communications to other points in the Islamic Empire. The river made Cairo a center of the trade between the Mediterranean and India.

Close to Cairo was its twin city, Fustat. A garrison town founded around 641 by Muslims, Fustat was another important and thriving Egyptian town. The two cities eventually merged.

Cordoba

Cordoba in southern Spain has a long history of being influenced by conquerors. The city was founded around the first century b.c.e. by the Romans. In 572, it was taken from the Romans by the Visigoths, a Germanic tribe. The Muslims seized it from the Visigoths in 711. In 756, Abd al-Rahman, the Umayyad prince who had escaped being slaughtered by the Abbasids, took control of Cordoba.

As the capital of the Umayyad amirs in Spain, Cordoba became the jewel of Europe. It was also a center of trade and industry in the area, and the city grew rich and prospered. It was famous for the production of silk and paper. Cordoban craftsmen were celebrated for a decorated crimson leather that came to be known—and is still known today—as cordovan.

Cordoba was also a center of learning and culture, not only for the Muslim world but for Europe as well. From Cordoba and other cities in Spain, poetry, science, philosophy, and medical knowledge spread throughout the Islamic Empire and into Europe. Scholars in Cordoba directly influenced European scholars, including such writers as St. Thomas

CONNECTIONS >>>>>>>>>>>>>>>>>>>>>>>>>>>>>>>>

Muslim Influence in Spain

At the height of the Islamic Empire, the Arabs controlled the southeastern two-thirds of the Iberian Peninsula. In addition to Cordoba, the Muslims revitalized such Spanish cities as Toledo, Granada, and Seville. For more than five centuries, Spain was a unique place in Europe, a region where culture and learning were valued and nurtured.

By 1248, when Seville was conquered by Christian forces, the Muslims had lost control of all of Spain, except Granada. The conquerors did not initially expel all the Muslims. By about 1500 though, after the fall of Granada, things had changed. In their attempts to wipe out all traces of Muslim influence, the Christian conquerors banned Arabic and Muslims in Spain were faced with the choice of conversion or exile. Despite this, Islamic influences can still be detected throughout the region. For example, many Arabic words are part of the Spanish language. The Spanish expression *olé* comes from the Arabic *wallahi*, which means "by God!" Many other Spanish words that begin with al

are Islamic in origin, including *alcachofa* (artichoke), *aldea* (village), and *aljibe* (well).

Visitors can also see remnants of Muslim control in Spanish architecture. The Alhambra in Granada (see page 46) and the Giralda Tower in Seville are two examples of the influence of Islamic style on the Iberian Peninsula. Many homes in southern Spain still retain such Muslim architectural touches as the use of whitewashed, windowless outer walls and central courtyards.

Many important goods were introduced to Europe via Muslim Spain. Sugar cane, cotton, rice, almonds, cured meats, and many types of fruits and vegetables all first came to Europe thanks to the Muslim conquerors. One of Muslim Spain's key contributions to Europe was the introduction of paper. The production of paper spread from China to the Middle East, then onward to Spain, Italy, and the rest of Europe. Paper-making enabled people to produce books more cheaply, and encouraged the spread of learning and knowledge throughout Europe.

Aquinas (1225-1274) and Dante Alighieri (1265-1321). Some historians believe that Dante based his *Divine Comedy* on Muhammad's journey from Jerusalem to Heaven.

By the early 900s, Cordoba was the largest city on the Iberian Peninsula, with as many as 500,000 people living there. Even Muslims from other parts of the empire believed Cordoba was one of the most beautiful cities in the Muslim world. Many who visited the city chose to relocate and make their homes there.

Cordoba remained under Muslim control until 1236, when it was conquered by Ferdinand of Castile (1199-1252), the king of Spain.

Trade and Industry

From the earliest days of the empire, trade was the most important industry. Not only were early Muslim merchants responsible for the wealth and prosperity of the empire, they also helped spread Islam, Arabic, and Arabian-Islamic culture. Kharijite merchants in North Africa, for example, helped spread their particular brand of Islam to the people there. As a result, the Kharijites are strongest in this area today.

At first, trade throughout the empire was primarily land-based. Caravans of camels laden with goods from India, Southeast Asia, and China trekked across the desert, carrying such items as grain, silk, cloth, wines, dried fruits, ivory, wood, perfume, and precious gems and metals. Trade in gold and slaves with Africa was also an important part of the merchant industry.

Western Europe, however, was of little importance as a trading partner. According to historian Bernard Lewis in *The Muslim Discovery of Europe*, exports from Europe were "too few and too insignificant" to deserve mention during the empire's earliest days.

The caravans traveled slowly, usually at about three miles an hour. At various points along the route, they could stop at a *caravanserai*, a sort of crude motel. Here, the caravan leader would find a room for himself and a place for his camels to rest, eat, and drink.

Caravans faced many obstacles, not the least of which was the hot, dry desert. Bandits were also common along some caravan routes. But merchants were quite willing to face the risks because of the huge profits involved. The wealthiest people in the early Islamic Empire were those engaged in successful trading ventures.

As the empire expanded, the demand for exotic goods from remote corners of the empire also grew. In addition, people in such large cities as

Baghdad required constant supplies of food and other trade items. The land trade was soon supplemented by the shipping trade. Merchant ships traveled from port to port, more quickly and easily transporting goods throughout the huge area controlled by the Muslims. Muslim traders may have operated as far north as the Baltic region and northern Europe.

As trade developed, there was a need for a standard currency and common banking practices. During the Abbasid Dynasty, two different types of currency were used: In the east, the Persian silver *dirham* was the standard of exchange, while the Byzantine gold *denarius* was used in the west. The value of these two currencies fluctuated relative to one another, just as the value of currency does today. To handle currency exchanges, money changers became common in bazaars and markets across the empire. As the money changer began lending funds and

Camel Highway
This modern camel caravan in Libya could be a scene from the Islamic Empire. Camels were often the most efficient way to transport goods across vast stretches of desert.

73

Check, Please

Banking and commerce in the Islamic Empire was more sophisticated than anything in Europe at the time—and for about three centuries to come. A number of Islamic banking concepts survive and are still used in the financial world today. For example, people throughout the empire understood the concept of credit. They wrote up special documents that could be cashed at a bank or any of its branches throughout the empire. These documents were called *sakk,* from which we get the word *check.*

Other Islamic contributions live on in words that we now use to describe commercial and financial ideas. For example, the word *average* comes from the Arabic word *awariyah,* meaning damaged goods. By the 17th century, the word had evolved to mean the fair distribution of losses due to damaged goods.

Another Arabic word still used in the business world is *tariff,* which is a tax on imported goods. During the Islamic Empire, tariffs were announcements or notifications that were posted so that merchants knew how much tax to pay the empire on cargoes of imported goods. And the word *carat,* which we use to describe the weight of precious metals and stones, comes from the Arabic word *qirat.* To merchants throughout the empire, *qirat* was a measure equal to one seed from a carob tree, or four grains. The seeds were used to balance a scale when weighing out gold.

offering letters of credit, his role evolved into that of a banker. Because the Quran forbids Muslims from lending money at interest, early bankers in the empire were usually Jewish or Christian—often operating with Muslim merchants as partners.

The Islamic Empire had many important port cities. One key port was Siraf, located on the eastern coast of the Persian Gulf. Foods from Oman and goods from Africa, India, and other areas arrived by *dhows,* small boats with triangular sails. The goods were then transported by camel caravans to other parts of the empire.

During the Abbasid Dynasty, Baghdad quickly became the most important trading city. Goods from all over the empire were shipped up the Tigris River. At the bazaars of Baghdad, people could purchase exotic foods and unusual trinkets. Here they might find porcelain, silk, and paper from China; gemstones from central Asia; and furs from Scandinavia. Baghdad was also an export center, with the empire's goods shipped out to lands far and wide.

Textile production was a major Islamic industry. In addition to damask (see the box on page 35), cities around the empire produced cloth made of silk, linen, cotton, flax, and wool. One special type of textile made in the empire was *tiraz,* cotton or linen cloth embroidered with passages from the Quran. The cloth was made in special workshops, also called *tiraz,* which were controlled by the caliph. Every piece made included the name and location of the workshop, the date, and the name of the current caliph.

Conquests and border wars made the business of making war a profitable one. Cordoba, for example, was home to workshops that manufactured thousands of tents, shields, bows, and arrows each year to supply the Islamic armies of conquest. War horses and camels to carry soldier's goods were also bred.

Craftsmen throughout the empire shared their skills with one another, and the technology of one area soon spread to another. Artisans from Baghdad, for example, ventured to Spain and North Africa to share their metal working techniques. From there, such skills as metal working, weaving, and leather tanning, eventually were transmitted throughout Europe.

Muslim conquests, unlike later Mongol invasions, did not destroy the existing towns and cities. When the Muslims conquered an area, they confiscated land only from the royals and their followers and did not disrupt the existing system of government. The Muslims understood that for them to profit from their newly conquered lands, they needed to allow life to continue as before.

Despite the measures taken to keep conquerors separate and different from the conquered, the language, religion, culture and social systems of the Arab Muslims had a profound influence on the lands they conquered. This began with Arabic, which was the official language of the empire and was required for all governmental transactions. To get along with those who held power—and to keep their jobs in the government—conquered peoples began learning to speak and write Arabic.

Other Religions

Although they expanded their empire in the name of religion, the Muslims tolerated other monotheistic religions. Christians, Jews, and Zoroastrians were allowed to continue worshiping as they chose. They were considered part of the social and religious category known as dhimmi (see page 61).

People who worshiped idols or multiple gods were not considered dhimmi. For them, the choice was to convert, leave the empire, or face death.

Soon, many of the conquered began to convert to Islam. Some dhimmis converted for financial reasons: They no longer wanted to pay the taxes that were levied on non-Muslims. Others, especially the poor and disadvantaged, embraced the Islamic notions of equality and justice. In this way, Islam spread throughout a vast empire that included people

CONNECTIONS >>>>>>>>>>>>

Dietary Restrictions

Muslims today must follow the same dietary laws that Muslims in the Islamic Empire followed. One such law forbids Muslims from eating pork. In addition, all meat must be slaughtered following specific rituals passed down through the centuries. This type of meat is called *halal*, which means "allowed" or "permitted" in Arabic. Most large U.S. cities today have halal butchers where Muslims can buy meat that has been prepared properly and has not come into contact with non-halal meat.

of many races, beliefs, and creeds. Intermarriage between Arab Muslims and non-Arabs also helped speed the process of assimilation.

Food and Shelter

From the eighth century to the 13th century, most citizens of the Islamic Empire enjoyed a good life, thanks to the wealth of the vast empire. Although early Arabs, particularly Bedouin tribes, generally lived on dates, milk, and the occasional bit of meat, this was no longer the case as the Muslims conquered new lands. As the empire expanded, Muslims were exposed to many exotic foods, and their diets became quite varied.

Cookbooks from the Islamic Empire still survive today, giving historians a glimpse into what its citizens ate. The first cookbook written in Arabic was compiled by Ibrahim ibn al-Mahdi (779–839), uncle of the caliph Mamun (r. 813–833). The book contained recipes for many gourmet dishes that were served to his nephew and the rest of the court, including a pureed eggplant and walnut dish and baked hen served on top of flatbread.

Muslims could buy all kinds of foods at the local bazaar. One type of shop, called a *harras*, sold ground meat that was combined with wheat and then fried. Other shops sold sauces, relishes, breads, and desserts.

Eggplant was probably the most common vegetable. It was used in a variety of dishes and could be prepared in many different ways. Lentils were also popular. However, only the wealthiest citizens ate such meats as lamb, chicken, or veal. Pork was not eaten, because Muslim dietary law forbids it.

Spices were an important part of the preparation of any meal. Popular cooking spices included cardamom, ginger, turmeric, and coriander. These spices gave Middle Eastern cuisine the distinct flavor it retains to this day. The Arabs introduced these spices to Europe.

Water was the drink of choice. Because of their desert roots, many Muslims considered water to be a source of life and purification. To give a person water, according to Muhammad, was an act deserving of the highest praise. The Muslims did enjoy other drinks, though. One was *sekanjabin*, water flavored with mint syrup. Water was also flavored with lemons, violets, roses, bananas, and many other sweet substances.

Despite the variety of foods available, dates retained their popularity and importance. These sweet, fleshy fruits from the date palm were served fresh or used to make other desserts. Dates were even used to make a type of alcoholic beverage called *khamr*, which was popular despite the Islamic prohibition on drinking alcohol.

Before a meal was served, it was important for all guests to wash their hands. A pitcher of water and a basin were always located near the table for this purpose. During the Abbasid Dynasty, food was brought out on big brass trays and set on a low table. Diners used their thumb and the first two fingers of their right hand to eat. It was considered bad manners to lick one's fingers.

The expansion of the empire brought a change of habitat for many Arabs. Although many Bedouins chose to continue living their nomadic desert lifestyle, others built permanent homes in the newly-conquered lands. For the wealthy, home consisted of a large single building with a central open courtyard. The courtyard often had a fountain or a garden in the center. In many cases, extended families lived together in these big houses, with different branches of the family residing in separate apartments.

Inside, the apartments contained little furniture. Ornate rugs

CONNECTIONS >>>>>>>>>>>>

Islamic Cuisine

Many people have heard the story that Italian explorer Marco Polo introduced pasta to Europe in 1298 after he returned from China. Several historians, however, believe that pasta was introduced into Italy centuries earlier—by Muslim invaders in Sicily. The first pasta—balls and strings of dried flour—may have been invented by Arab conquerors in their quest to find a food that could be easily transported from battle to battle.

Another important food contribution was sugar cane. This popular sweetener first came to Europe from the Islamic Empire, and it was one of the top commodities traded until the 18th century. With the introduction of sugar cane to Europe, sweets of all sorts quickly became popular. The words *candy, caramel, marzipan, sherbet, sugar,* and *syrup* are all Arabic in origin.

Other culinary contributions that we still eat today include flat breads, which were popular and eaten with most meals. In the United States, these flat breads take the form of pita and wraps. Other Middle Eastern foods that made their way to Europe and other parts of the world include falafel (ground chickpeas and spices that are shaped into balls and fried) and hummus, a kind of dip also made with chickpeas and spices.

or cushions were thrown over small square mattresses for the family to sit on. Floor coverings were important to Muslims. Both practical and decorative, rugs served as places for prayer, rest, eating, and entertaining. In mosques, at home, or as decorations for a royal palace, carpets were highly prized. The caliph Harun al-Rashid had 22,000 rugs in his palace.

Even before Islam, carpets were important and multi-functional belongings. They were used not only as cushions, blankets, and pillows when the nomad was at home in his tent, but were also useful during travel. Rugs could be thrown across the back of a camel or horse or used as saddle bags to carry possessions.

Some rugs were huge works of art that took months, even years, to create. They might include distinctive ornamental patterns such as outlines of flowers, foliage, fruit or geometric patterns (collectively known today as arabesque, which means "in the manner of Arabs"), created by the careful placement and tying of thousands of knots.

Silk Carpet
Intricately woven rugs were highly prized in the Empire, and still are today. They ranged in size from huge works of art to small rugs to kneel on during prayer.

Pictures of gardens were also popular. Particularly spectacular rugs might also be hung on the walls. Rugs were made of every fiber from wool to silk. Some were even woven with silver and gold thread and studded with gemstones.

One common use for rugs was in prayer. Prayer rugs, large enough for one person, could be carried to and from the mosque or laid down wherever the person was, making it easier to kneel in worship. Prayer rugs often had a *mihrab* woven into them, with a rectangle above that the prayer could touch his forehead to. Other decorations might include items commonly found in the mosque, such as hanging lanterns, archways, and Quranic inscriptions.

Mosaic tiles, an art borrowed from the Byzantine Empire, were popular and often graced floors and walls. Mosaic tiles were especially popular with the Seljuk Turks. They were used to cover walls, ceilings, and floors in mosques, bath houses, private homes, and royal palaces. Later, during the Abbasid Dynasty, the *diwan*, a sofa that stretched along three sides of the room, became popular. Today, another word for sofa is *divan*, which specifically means a long, backless sofa with pillows, set against a wall.

Style

The early Bedouin people wore simple clothes designed to protect themselves from the scorching rays of the desert sun. Their clothing consisted of a long shirt with a sash (sash is an Arabic word) and a flowing upper garment.

As the empire expanded, the basic style of clothing remained the same, with some refinements. Women and men alike continued to wear long shirts that covered the upper part of the body. Beneath this tunic they wore loose pants. Women covered their heads with long, flowing scarves and veils, while men often wore cloaks around their shoulders. These cloaks were multi-functional, serving as a rain or sun shield, a blanket, or a sack to carry goods.

Islamic men, like women, also covered their heads. Many used pieces of cloth that could be wrapped around the head in many different ways, similar to today's turban.

The courtiers of the Abbasid Dynasty introduced many new styles to the empire. During warmer weather, silk gowns became the fashion. In colder weather, quilted clothing was popular.

Islamic men at court often dyed their beards with henna to

CONNECTIONS >>>>>>>>>>>

Persian Carpets

Today, "Persian carpets," or rugs from the East, are still popular in American homes as furnishings and works of art. Because of the great care that often goes into maintaining these rugs, many still exist from the late 1800s and 1900s. People buy patterned carpets that are brand new or very old.

Oriental rugs are still manufactured in the same regions where they were made centuries ago. Traditional rug-making areas include Iran, Turkey, Central Asia, and India. In keeping with early Islamic traditions, most oriental rugs contain symmetrical patterns and designs. Many of the traditional designs on what we today call Persian rugs came from Islamic carpet makers more than 1,000 years ago.

redden them. This was a custom that dated back to the time of Muhammad. They also trimmed their hair to reveal their necks and ears.

Cosmetics were used in the court of the Abbasid caliphs. Women used black kohl under their eyes to accentuate the size of their eyes. They also dyed their fingertips with henna to redden them. Perfumes were popular too, for men and women alike. Men, for example, sometimes scented their beards before dining. Rosewater was a favorite scent.

The Abbasid caliphs' wives often set fashion trends that were followed by Muslim women. One wife decorated her shoes with gemstones—a fashion that has endured to this day. Another, to cover a blemish on her forehead, designed a jeweled, lacy veil that quickly became the latest rage among Baghdad women. Abbasid women also wore anklets, bracelets, and other pieces of jewelry.

Cleanliness was extremely important to the people of the Islamic Empire. While people in Europe believed that bathing was dangerous and unhealthy, the people of the empire believed in rubbing the body with pleasant-smelling lotions, cleaning the teeth with a stick and paste, and using perfumes to mask foul body and other odors.

Public baths were particularly popular, especially during the Abbasid Dynasty. Baghdad alone had thousands of them. The baths had hot and cold running water; the hot water was heated by huge hearths. Bathers used ground ashes as soap. The public baths provided social opportunities, giving Islamic men the chance to relax with other Islamic men. They also gave Islamic women one of their rare opportunities to get out of the house and socialize with other women.

CONNECTIONS >>>>>>>>>>>>

The Mattress Comes to Europe

One of the new ideas brought back to Europe by Crusaders was the mattress. The Crusaders borrowed the Arabic practice of sleeping on pillows, cushions, and rugs thrown upon the floor. Before that, common people slept on piles of straw, tree boughs, or similar material heaped in a corner of their house. The word *mattress* comes from the Arabic word *matrah*, which means a place where something is thrown.

Women and Family Life

Throughout the Islamic Empire, marriage was considered a sacred institution and, for men, a duty. Men usually married for the first time around the age of 20, while women were sometimes as young as 12. Families generally arranged the marriages, with the husband's family giving the bride a dowry, which was hers to keep.

CONNECTIONS >>

Keeping Clean in the Islamic Empire

For the Arab people, the concern for good physical hygiene may have originated thousands of years ago: Archaeologists digging in Babylon (now southern Iraq) discovered a soap-like substance in clay jars dating back to about 2800 b.c.e. These early concoctions, made with fat and ashes, may have been used to clean clothing.

During the height of the Islamic Empire, the Arabs pioneered the use of hard soap made out of olive oil, alkali, and natron, a type of salt. Under Muslim control, Italy and Spain became soap-making centers. From here, soap was exported to other parts of Europe.

Muslims in Spain and Italy also helped popularize the connection between cleanliness and health. Muslim doctors put forth many theories regarding the role that poor hygiene played in sickness and the spread of illness. *Hammamat*, or bathhouses, were believed to play a key role in preventing contagious diseases from spreading. They were even known as "silent doctors." Inspectors carefully examined each *hammam* to make sure it was kept clean. Today, *hammamat* are still found throughout the Middle East. Many are attached to mosques.

The Muslims also popularized dental hygiene. Although they did not invent the toothbrush or toothpaste, Muslim doctors helped advance knowledge of the mouth and teeth, and the need to keep them clean.

According to the Quran, men were allowed to have up to four wives, while women could have just one husband. However, the husband had to treat each wife equally and be able to afford to take care of all of his wives. This meant providing each wife with her own quarters, her own cooking and sleeping areas, and her own slaves. Most Islamic men had just one wife at a time.

After the death of Khadija, Muhammad himself practiced polygamy—having more than one wife. He was allowed as many wives as he liked, and at one time had nine wives. Although he married most of his wives for political reasons, he also married for love. Muhammad was the first Muslim to create a *harem*, or restricted place, for his wives. The wives were separated from other people so that they could not be held to blame for impious or scandalous behavior.

Each wife lived in her own small apartment. When male visitors came to the house, a curtain called the *hijab* was put up to prevent them from seeing Muhammad's wives. But the hijab gradually came to mean more than a curtain. Eventually it became the custom followed by Muslim women of wearing a veil, head covering, and modest dress in public, including covering their arms and legs. Hijab, meaning modest attire, is still worn by most Muslim women today. The word hijab also refers to the veil and head covering itself.

The Quran made other important changes in the life of Arab women. Not only could they now keep their dowries even if their husband divorced them, but the Quran stipulated that a man must treat his wife kindly. Islamic law also allowed women to inherit and own property, separate from male family members.

The first duty of women throughout the empire was to care for the home and their families. At home, some women had their own small businesses, especially spinning or dyeing cloth. Because they could not bring their goods to the marketplace, they had to hire men to sell their goods on their behalf.

Wealthier women had more freedom than did ordinary Muslim women. In some cases, they were able to attend school and take up a profession. Some wealthy Muslim women, for example, practiced medicine and operated as merchants. These wealthy women had slaves who took care of their household chores for them.

Men were under no restrictions to remain at home. For entertainment, they could go to the public baths, play chess with their friends, or hang out at the local tavern. Although alcohol was forbidden, taverns served a fermented liquid called *nabidh*, made from raisins or dates. At the tavern, the men might be entertained by music or poetry recitations. However, at home there were restrictions on whom men could socialize with (particularly in the homes of non-relatives). Women usually had more freedom than men to socialize in private homes.

For children, education began at home. From an early age, children were taught to memorize passages from the Quran. As they grew older, the Quran and the Hadith were used to teach them to read. Later, boys would receive more formal lessons at mosques, schools, or Islamic centers. During the Abbasid Dynasty, boys usually began attending mosque schools at around the age of seven—as long as their families could afford to pay a small tuition.

Wealthier boys continued their education longer. They might attend seminars, discuss poetry, and read classic works of Greek that had been translated into Arabic. These lessons prepared the wealthy young men for positions of importance. The empire's first universities were founded in the 10th century under the Abbasid Dynasty.

CONNECTIONS >>>>>>>>>>>>>>>>>>>>>>>>>>>>>>>>

Fun and Games

Chess was the caliph's game of choice; he even held chess championships at the palace. While this game of strategy had come to Persia from India, it was introduced to Europe by the Muslims. The term *checkmate*, which in chess means one player has cornered the other's king, comes from the Arabic phrase *shah mat*, meaning "the king is dead."

Other games borrowed from the Persians and popularized by the Muslims include polo and backgammon—both of which are still played today.

Two Abbasid caliphs, Al Mahdi and Al Hadi, were responsible for the construction of a large number of libraries and centers of education in Baghdad. Scientists and scholars from all over the empire went to the capital to teach and learn in the universities (also known as "houses of knowledge") and *madrasas* (Islamic schools).

It Is Good to Be the Caliph

The ruling dynasty—especially the Abbasids—lived a much different life than did the average Muslim in the Islamic Empire. As the Abbasid caliphs relinquished their control over the government to others, they turned to a life of rituals, pleasure, and entertainment.

The caliph was almost constantly surrounded by courtiers. Those who wished to meet with the caliph had to kneel down in front of the ruler and kiss the floor. During the early Abbasid Dynasty, a leather carpet was kept unrolled before the caliph's throne; if need be, the royal executioner

Circumcision

One tradition practiced by many cultures, including Muslims throughout the empire, was male circumcision—removal of the foreskin of the penis. Muslim boys were usually circumcised around the age of 10. Although not part of Islamic law, circumcision was considered a sacred rite. One caliph who clearly thought the practice important was Fatimid caliph al-Muizz. In 962, the caliph held a circumcision festival. During the month-long festival, all boys of the right age in his domain had to come and be circumcised along with the caliph's three sons. Thousands of boys were circumcised during this festival. The boys and their families were rewarded with money and gifts.

In some areas, girls were also circumcised—the clitoris was removed. This practice, which is not Muslim in origin, continues in some countries today and is very controversial. It is a far more radical and painful procedure than male circumcision, causes mutilation of the genitals, results in lasting pain, and poses a risk of infection and serious medical problems.

could step up, lop off the head of anyone who displeased the royal leader, then take the dead body away without making a mess. The executioner was always ready, with his sword drawn, to obey the caliph's signal.

How could a courtier stay out of trouble? According to vizier Nizam al-Mulk (d. 1092), the perfect courtier should always agree with everything the caliph had to say and:

> [S]hould be essentially honorable and of excellent character, of cheerful disposition and irreproachable in respect of his religion, discreet and a clean liver. He should be able to tell a story and repeat a narrative either humorous or grave, and he should remember news. He should also be consistently a carrier of pleasant tidings and the announcer of felicitous happenings. He should also have acquaintance of backgammon and chess, and if he can play a musical instrument and can handle a weapon, it is all the better. (Quoted in *Medieval Islamic Sourcebook* at www.fordham.edu/halsall/source/640hangedpoems.html)

The Abbasids enjoyed many different entertainments. Musicians and poets were very popular at court, and the most talented ones often received subsidies from the caliph. Another popular pastime was hunting. The caliph, on horseback, used dogs, falcons, ferrets, and even cheetahs to help him track wild game.

As might be expected, dining was a grand experience at the palace. Under the caliph Mamun (783-833), diners were feted with perishable foods from far away that were shipped in lead boxes packed with snow. Mamun's guests were also the first Arabs to dine using tables and chairs instead of sitting on the floor. The caliph's tables were made of gold and silver.

Harems became more common during the Abbasid Dynasty. In addition to their four wives allowed by Quranic law, caliphs kept hundreds—sometimes thousands—of concubines. Concubines might be female slaves or prisoners of war who caught the caliph's eye. To guard the women, eunuchs (castrated slaves) were often employed.

CONNECTIONS >>>>>>>>>>>>>>>>

Salukis:
The Dogs of Caliphs

The Saluki is one of the oldest-known breeds of domesticated dogs. Thousands of years ago, Bedouin tribes used the sharp-eyed and lightning-fast Salukis, also known as gazelle hounds, to hunt gazelle and other animals. The dogs were so highly prized that they were even allowed to sleep in the tents of their masters.

In ancient Egypt, the dogs were kept by pharaohs and became known as the "royal dogs of Egypt." Only royalty were allowed to keep the animals, and a favorite dog might be mummified and placed in his master's tomb. After the rise of the Islamic Empire, the dogs became popular as the pets of the caliphs. They accompanied the caliph on hunting expeditions, and were often given to friends and important people as signs of royal favor and esteem.

Salukis are sleek, silky animals who hunt by sight and are part of a group of dogs known as sighthounds. Like Greyhounds, they are swift and intelligent animals. In some countries, Salukis are raced against one another.

Holidays

Throughout the empire, Muslims observed several religious and secular celebrations. The most important religious holiday throughout the kingdom was Eid al-Adha (the feast of sacrifice). The holiday marked the end of the sacred pilgrimage to Mecca. On the 10th day of Dhul-Hijjah (the final month of the Islamic calendar), an animal was sacrificed and prayers were offered. During the rest of the four-day holiday, Muslims feasted and visited family.

Another major religious holiday, Eid al-Fitr (the feast of breaking fast), marked the end of the fast of Ramadan. Under the Abbasid Dynasty, long processions were organized, followed by a huge feast that might last up to three days. At the feast, diners ate such specially-prepared dishes as thin pancakes, breads, and dried fruits. On the streets of Baghdad, citizens were entertained by musicians and poets.

One secular holiday enjoyed by the Fatimids in North Africa was Nawruz, a festival that had its roots in ancient Iran. During Nawruz, some Muslims celebrated the return of spring. The celebration included

The Zamzam Well

The Zamzam well is located in Mecca, a few yards east of the Kaaba. It is 115 feet deep and is topped by an elegant dome.

Muslims believe that Allah created the well to provide for Hagar, a wife of the Biblical figure Abraham (the Judeo-Christian Bible says Hagar was a servant in Abraham's household), who was the mother of Ishmael. When Hagar was forced to leave Abraham's household, she and her baby son wandered in the desert and eventually were overcome with thirst. In her desperate search for water, Hagar ran seven times back and forth between the two hills of Safa and Marwa. Then, in despair, she sat down and waited to die. Allah saw her effort and miraculously blessed the spot with a spring.

Muslims on the hajj recall this event by circling the same hills seven times, and by drinking the water of Zamzam. It is said to be able to satisfy both thirst and hunger. Pilgrims to Mecca collect the water in bottles to bring home relatives and friends who are ill, because it is also said to have healing powers.

dancing, bonfires, and giving gifts to friends and family. It was also customary to give a gift to the caliph. However, some religious scholars felt that good Muslims should not celebrate this holiday, because of its secular roots.

Death and Burial

The Quran offers Muslims hope of an afterlife. According to Islamic belief, the soul, freed from the body, moves on to a new phase. Those who have lived a righteous life are rewarded with heaven, while those who have not are consigned to hell.

When a Muslim died, the body was first washed to purify it. Then it was wrapped in a seamless white shroud that had been dipped during a pilgrimage into the waters of Mecca's Zamzam well (see the box on page 86). Throughout these preparations, passages from the Quran were recited over the body. Finally, the body was buried on its side, facing Mecca. Martyrs–those who had died in the cause of Islam–were to be buried as they died, with no washing or other preparation.

All Muslims had to be buried the morning after their death. During the burial, women–sometimes paid professional mourners–cried out in grief for the dead person. Mourners wore bands of cloth around their head as a symbol of their grief. Because Muhammad opposed fancy memorials to the dead, most Muslim graves were simple and plain, often without a coffin. However, wealthy Muslims were often buried in large, domed tombs.

The last words spoken at the grave during burial were also the first words the dead person had heard as an infant: "There is no god but Allah, and Muhammad is his Prophet."

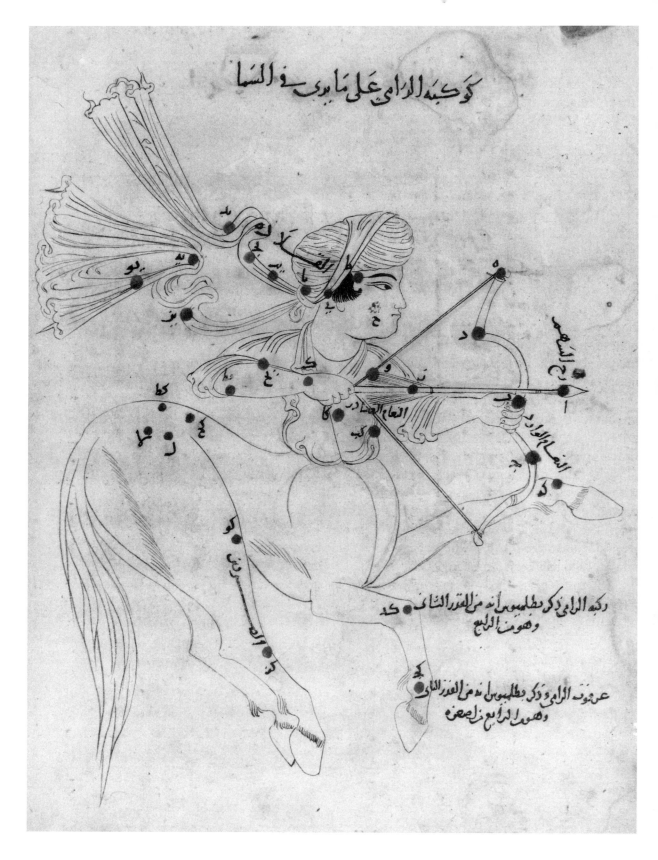

CHAPTER 6

Islamic Art, Science, and Culture

THE ISLAMIC EMPIRE WAS THE MOST ADVANCED CIVILIZATION of its time. Much of what historians think of as Islamic culture was not Arabian in origin, however. Learning, science, and customs were all influenced by the people the Muslims conquered. Jews, Christians, and Hindus, Greeks, Persians, and Africans all contributed to the development of what we know as Islamic culture. As the empire grew, the conquerors incorporated new elements into their own civilization, often improving upon the originals.

There were, of course, two major Arab contributions to Islamic culture: religion and the Arabic language. The language of the conquerors, Arabic became the language of government and learning. It replaced Persian, Greek, and many other languages throughout the empire. Conquered people who wanted to succeed under their new rulers quickly learned Arabic. As a result, Arabic served as a powerful cultural unifier.

Islamic culture first blossomed during the Umayyad Dynasty. The Umayyads were heavily influenced by Arab traditions. The empire's true golden age, however, came during the Abbasid Dynasty. The years 786 to 809, under Harun al-Rashid, were especially fruitful. Muslim cities became centers of world culture.

Scholars throughout the empire learned about science and philosophy by reading the works of the ancient Greeks. But ancient Greek itself was not a widely known language. The first people to translate these works were mainly Jews and Christians in Syria. The works of Aristotle (384–322 B.C.E.), Euclid (flourished in the 300s B.C.E.), Galen (c. 130–200 B.C.E.), Hippocrates (c. 460–370 B.C.E.), Plato (c. 427–347 B.C.E.), and Ptolemy (flourished in the second century) were all translated into

OPPOSITE
The Age of Sagittarius
This drawing from the book Forms of the Fixed Stars *by Abdulrahman al-Sufi shows the constellation Sagittarius. The book dates from 1009–1010.*

Syriac (the language of Syria) and then into Arabic. Thanks to the Arabic translations of the Greek masters, preserved in vast libraries throughout the Islamic Empire, Europe was eventually exposed to these important works of mathematics, astronomy, and logic. Not all of the Greeks were considered worthy of translation, however. The works of playwrights and poets, including Homer (before 700 B.C.E.) and Sophocles (c. 496–406 B.C.E.), were not considered practical or important.

Sacred Texts

Before the empire, the peoples of Arabia relied mainly upon oral recitation to preserve their literature and history. But as the empire grew, great works of literature were written. The most famous is the Quran, the sacred text of Islam. There were also other important pieces composed during the six centuries of the empire, including beautiful poetry and humorous prose. Literature composed throughout the course of the empire continues to be read and appreciated today.

The Quran is the most important and earliest piece of Arabic prose writing (although it also has some poetic elements). For Muslims, the book is more than just a piece of literature—it is a way of life. The Quran is the written record of the messages Muhammad received directly from God. The messages were not written down by Muhammad, however, but were transcribed after his death by people who had heard him reciting and explaining God's word. The most important message of the Quran is that there is only one God.

Written in Arabic, the holy book is divided into 114 chapters called suras. Except for the first one, which is an exhortation to God, the suras are ordered from longest to shortest; no one could be sure about the order in which Muhammad received these messages from God.

In the early 650s, during the reign of Uthman, a standard edition of the Quran was compiled and approved. Many historians consider this to be Uthman's chief achievement. All other versions of the Quran were ordered destroyed, although some did survive.

Second in importance to the Quran is the Hadith. The Hadith, which means "narrative," is a collection of the sayings and deeds of Muhammad, compiled almost two centuries after his death. The Hadith contains the Sunna, or tradition, of Muhammad's teachings, speeches, and actions, and is an important reference for how good Muslims should think and act. Since the first parts of the Hadith written down in the late 800s, this collection has guided Islamic politics, religion, and law.

After the death of Muhammad, stories of his words and deeds were passed down orally from person to person. Beginning in the late eighth century, religious scholars began trying to authenticate the various collections of Hadith by researching the chain of people who had told each story. As the scholars researched the roots of each story, they weeded out tales that could not be traced to trustworthy tellers. To prove their authenticity, each Hadith begins with an *isnad*, or list of the people who transmitted the tale. The ideal Hadith can be traced back to a family member or companion of Muhammad.

Poetry

People of the Arabian Peninsula had a love for the spoken word. A Bedouin proverb (quoted by Philip K. Hitti in the book *The Arabs: A Short History*) says, "The beauty of man lies in the eloquence of his tongue." In each tribe, tales were

CONNECTIONS >>>>>>>>>>>>

Umar al-Khayyam

Umar al-Khayyam (c. 1048–1125) was a Persian Muslim mathematician and astronomer. A true Renaissance man centuries before the European Renaissance, Umar helped create an accurate solar calendar and was the first person to solve cubic equations. He gained his greatest fame, however, as a poet. Throughout his life, he composed more than 1,000 quatrains—poems in which the stanzas are made up of four lines each. These poems were collected in the *Rubaiyyat of Omar Khayyam*.

In 1859, Umar's masterpiece was translated into English. The poems rapidly gained popularity throughout the West, and are among the best-known works of poetry around the world. Many of Umar's poems, including the following, talk about making the most of life. (The excerpt below is from the fifth edition of British author Edward FitzGerald's translation.)

The Moving Finger writes; and having writ,
Moves on: nor all your Piety nor Wit
Shall lure it back to cancel half a Line,
Nor all your Tears wash out a Word of it.

told that had been memorized and handed down from generation to generation. These stories celebrated the bravery of the tribe, related tales of its heroes, and ridiculed its enemies.

Each tribe had its own poet who was not only the storehouse of tribal history and legends, but also often acted as the clan's spokesman. In pre-Islamic Mecca, poetry contests pitted the clans' chief poets against one another.

One early form of Arabic poetry was the *qasida*, or long-metered ode. The qasida had three parts: the prologue, the journey, and the eulogy or invective. These odes told of desert journeys that took the narrator away from the people he loved, and his sense of sorrow at the separation. The qasida continued to be popular even after conquest began.

Some of these poems were written by Arabs who yearned for their old lives in the desert.

In the early eighth century, Muslims learned the art of papermaking from Chinese captives. As paper became more readily available throughout the empire, the written word flourished. Before long, libraries to house these new works were being built in all the major cities.

Some of the best poems, both long and short, were hung on the walls of the Kaaba, where Muhammad allowed them to remain after he returned to Mecca. Today, these poems are known as the Hanged Poems. The overall structure of the poem was considered less important than the craftsmanship of each individual line, and each line is a work of art in itself. As a result, these poems are sometimes called "strings of pearls."

Many of the caliphs patronized poets. A common Islamic expression, "cutting off the tongue" of a poet, meant supporting the poet with money to prevent him from writing nasty poems about a person.

Two of the most important poets of the empire were Abu Nuwas (c. 750–810) and Mutanabbi (915–965). Abu Nuwas wrote about love and wine, and was famous for his use of language and his love of imagery. He was also famous for his drinking songs. One line of his poetry read, "Accumulate as many sins as you can."

Mutanabbi was famous for his qasida, as well as poems praising his patrons in flowery and highly descriptive language. His sarcastic political poems, however, often landed him in hot water.

Even some of the caliphs dabbled in poetry. Caliph Yazid composed a poem to his father that described how angry his father would become when Yazid was drinking.

Poem of Zuhair

The Poem of Zuhair is one of the Hanged Poems that was posted on the walls of the Kaaba. The poem is long, with each line able to stand on its own. The following are some excerpts, as posted on Fordham University's Medieval Islamic Sourcebook website.

He who is possessed of plenty, and is miserly with his great wealth toward his people, will be dispensed with, and abused.

He who keeps his word, will not be reviled; and he whose heart is guided to self-satisfying benevolence will not stammer.

And he who dreads the causes of death, they will reach him, even if he ascends the tracts of the heavens with a ladder.

And he who shows kindness to one not deserving it, his praise will be a reproach against him, and he will repent of having shown kindness...

And whatever of character there is in a man, even though he thinks it concealed from people, it is known...

Many silent ones you see, pleasing to you, but their excess in wisdom or deficiency will appear at the time of talking.

The following excerpt is from Yazid's poem, as posted on the Cartage web site.

> *'Twas sweet the flowing cup to seize,*
> *'Tis sweet thy rage to see;*
> *And first I drink myself to please;*
> *And next—to anger thee.*

Prose

Contact with other cultures influenced Islamic literature, but style continued to be more important than form. For Islamic writers, the beauty of word and thought was of the utmost importance. The earliest prose pieces in the Islamic Empire were translations of Persian works about the life and manners of courtiers. Later, the Muslims developed their own prose forms. As time passed, prose eventually became the most important way of recording the history and stories of the Islamic Empire.

One important form of Islamic literature is the *sira*, which is a biography of Muhammad. The first sira was written by ibn Ishaq (c. 704–773), and it remains one of the few full biographies of Muhammad.

A type of purely entertaining literature called *adab* was enjoyed by citizens throughout the empire. Adab combined engaging tales with an educational lesson or moral. One of the first adab was Kalila and Dimna (750), a translation of some Indian fables. The tales, which were translated by ibn al Mukaffa during the reign of the caliph al-Mansur, used animals to teach lessons to those who would rule. Unfortunately, the author was not as pleasing as the work. Al-Mansur ordered the writer killed after he supported an uncle who rebelled against the caliph.

Another popular type of literature was the *maqama*, or "literary assembly." Maqamat were adventures, told by a fictional narrator, using rhymed prose. Writers used maqamat as a way to criticize conditions in the world around them and impart moral lessons, such as, "The worst of men is he whose today falls short of his yesterday." Like poetry, the form of the maqama was more important than its content. As a record of what life was like in the medieval Islamic Empire, this form of literature has had a lasting impact.

Art

The art of the Islamic Empire was unique, beautiful, and functional. Much of early Islamic art was created to beautify religious or everyday items. As in so many things, the Arabs were influenced by the other cultures

Thousand and One Nights

The best-known piece of literature to come out of the Islamic Empire, for Westerners, is the *Thousand and One Nights*. Also known as the *Arabian Nights*, the work is a collection of tales written by different authors over hundreds of years. The *Thousand and One Nights* gives a glimpse into what life was like in the Islamic Empire from the ninth through the 16th centuries.

The stories in the book include fairy tales from India and Persia, love stories from Egypt, and legends from Arabia. The tales from other countries and cultures were adapted by the authors to reflect Muslim traditions and customs. Familiar characters from the book include Ali Baba, Sinbad, and Aladdin. Although the work was widely read in the West after its translation into English in the 1840s, the *Thousand and One Nights* was not considered a great literary work by Muslims.

One of the most famous stories in the *Thousand and One Nights* is the story of Sinbad the sailor and his seven sea voyages. The story stems from ancient Persian folktales that were passed on orally for generations. The tale of Sinbad offers a glimpse into Islamic trade during the eighth and ninth centuries. In the book *The Arabs: A Short History*, Philip Hitti writes that some of Sinbad's adventures were based on actual reports of trading voyages made by Islamic merchants.

During his travels to India and other parts of the world, Sinbad experiences many wild and fantastic adventures. He is shipwrecked by a huge whale, attacked by a gigantic bird, and nearly squeezed to death by an enormous snake. He even dines with cannibals and lives to tell the tale. Sinbad eventually returns to Baghdad and becomes a wealthy merchant.

Today, the tale of Sinbad remains popular among people of all ages. The story has been turned into cartoons, movies, and books. The most recent version of the centuries-old tale was the animated Disney film *Sinbad*, released in 2003. Brad Pitt supplied Sinbad's voice.

they came into contact with during the conquest. In fact, there was no true Arab art form (other than poetry) before the expansion of the empire.

As a key force in all aspects of life in the Islamic empire, religion had a strong influence on art. During the early days of the empire, sculptures and images of people were prohibited in mosques and discouraged in general. Although these restrictions eased in later years, Muhammad was often depicted with his face covered and surrounded by a halo of flames. More commonly, images of people were found in such non-religious settings as bathhouses and harems. They were also more acceptable on pillows and carpets.

Two of the most common types of Islamic visual art were calligraphy and illuminated manuscripts. Calligraphy, which is the art of elegant, ornamental writing, was the most respected of all the Islamic art forms. Nothing was more worthy than to write the word of Allah, which was considered an act of worship in itself. Over the centuries, copies of the Quran have given Islamic calligraphers an opportunity to produce some of their finest and most beautiful works of art. These copies were often decorated with floral and geometric patterns and panels between each chapter.

Those who wanted to excel at calligraphy studied for years under a master calligrapher. The master taught his students how to sit in a squatting position when writing, with the paper balanced on one knee. Students were taught one of the six classic styles of rounded Arabic writing. One of the most important parts of being a calligrapher was learning how to properly cut a reed to make a pen. Pens were so important that they were sometimes passed on from masters to favorite students. They also learned how to make ink out of indigo, soot, and henna and how to line paper. Artists could make a profession of calligraphy, making copies of the Quran, government documents, books for libraries, and even writing inscriptions on mosques, palaces, and tombs.

Illumination is the art of creating brightly-colored miniature pictures. These miniatures were most commonly used to illustrate non-religious manuscripts. The first illuminations were used in Arabic translations of Greek works, and include pictures of plants, herbs, and animals from fables. Illumination was especially popular in Persia, Turkey, and India.

Copied by Hand
Islamic calligraphers turned the pages of the Quran into works of art. This 13th-century manuscript is from Morocco, and shows sura 176.

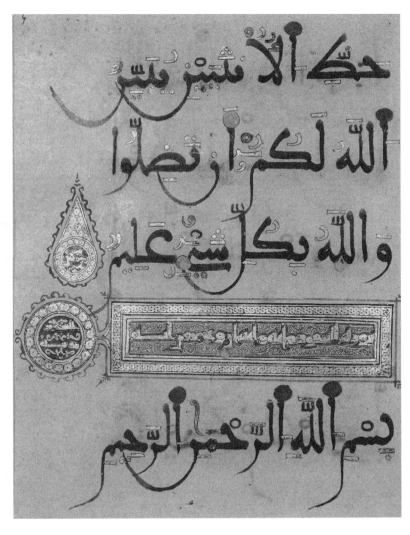

The Muslims also adopted the art forms of conquered peoples, particularly the use of decorative mosaics (see page 79) and carpet making (see page 78). Other art forms that originally came from outside the empire include pottery, ivory and wood carving, metal working with brass, bronze, gold, silver and copper; and glass making. Beginning in the ninth century, ceramics became quite popular. Inspired by the fine Chinese porcelain that passed along Islamic trade routes, artists began creating finely-decorated plates, vases, and jugs. A luster finish was very popular for these ceramic pieces. This was created by coating the pottery with metal oxides that, after being heated, took on a metallic shimmer. This process, called lustring, was eventually passed on to the west via Spain.

Music

Most forms of Islamic music developed during the eighth through 10th centuries. As the empire grew, Arabian music was influenced by the new cultures. Syria, Egypt, Persia, and later Spain were especially influential.

CONNECTIONS >>>>>>>>>>>>>>>>>>>>>>>>>>>>>>>>>

An Egyptian belly dancer performs at a private party.

"Oriental Dance"

For some American women, belly dancing has become a way to have fun and keep fit. Belly dancing, also known as *raks sharki*, or "oriental dance," has its roots in Arabia. There is some mystery, however, surrounding when and why *raks sharki* was first performed—particularly given the Islamic custom of modest dress for women. Some stories tell that the dance dates back to pre-Islamic days, when it was performed at weddings and other celebrations. Others believe the dance may have developed as a way for pregnant women to prepare their abdominal muscles for labor and birth. In some Islamic countries today, *raks sharki* is banned or discouraged.

Although the style of Arab music remained the same in many ways, it also borrowed aspects of the music from other areas. For this reason, classical Islamic music from Turkey is recognizably different from classical music from Morocco, Egypt, and other areas.

Islamic musicians were also heavily influenced by the ancient Greeks. As Greek works were translated into Arabic, music became revered as a science, similar to mathematics and astronomy. Arab scholars studied music, wrote treatises on it, and even created new theories of pitch, scales, and other technical aspects of music.

Despite the protests of conservative Muslims, who believed music was discouraged by Muhammad, music flourished in the royal courts of both the Umayyads and the Abbasids. Many musicians, like poets, were supported by the caliph and his court. Gifted musicians could earn fame and fortune throughout the empire.

One of the most famous musicians of the Islamic Empire was Ziryab (759–857), a freed slave from Baghdad who moved to Cordoba. In Spain, Ziryab became a renowned singer, teacher, and oud player (see page 47). He was well-rewarded for his skills: The amir Abd al-Rahman II (788–852) gave Ziryab his own furnished mansion, gifts, and a monthly salary. The famous musician combined Greek, Persian, and Arab influences in his compositions to create a style of music that was unique to Spain.

The distinctive musical sound that is associated with Arabia is the result of the musical instruments that were first used throughout the Islamic Empire. The main instrument for music-making in the empire was the oud. Known as "the king of musical instruments" and the "prince of enchantment," the oud may have originated in Egypt or in the Sassanian Empire. The oud, a forerunner of the lute, was a pear-shaped instrument with a rounded back and a flat front. Early ouds, made of lightweight wood, had four strings made of silk or animal gut.

The oud was held like a guitar and played with one or two picks that were attached to the forefinger. These picks were often made of trimmed eagle's feathers. The oud was the only instrument to accompany the sawt, a type of song that was eventually spread into Western Europe by crusaders returning from the Empire. The sawt, in which the audience chanted parts of a song in response to the singer, influenced troubadours, poet-musicians in Spain and France. The oud, which produced a deep sound, may even have been played on the battlefield.

Another stringed instrument used in Arabic music-making was the qanun, a zither-like instrument descended from the Egyptian harp.

Developed in the 10th century, the qanun was a flat, trapezoidal wooden board with 25 to 27 sets of strings made from animal gut or silk. This versatile instrument was played by plucking the strings with the fingers or with pieces of horn.

Percussion instruments included the *darbukkah*, or *tablah*, a small hand-held drum made by stretching goat, calf, or fish skin over a large clay container. The *mihbaj* was a multi-functional Bedouin instrument that doubled as a coffee grinder. The mihbaj was about a foot tall, with a two-foot tall pestle used both for grinding coffee and making percussion sounds.

The *nay* was a simple reed pipe, similar to a flute, adapted from the Sumerians. The nay most often had six holes in the front, with one hole underneath for the thumb. It was one the few wind instruments used in the Islamic Empire. During a performance, musicians might use as many as seven nays of different sizes to produce a variety of pitches and sounds.

Architecture

One of the most enduring legacies of the Islamic Empire is the unique and distinctive architecture that still survives in many regions today. And the most important architectural achievement throughout the duration of the empire was the mosque. For Muslims in the Islamic Empire, the mosque served as a place to worship Allah and much more. It was also the heart of the community. The mosque was a court of justice, a place for study, and even a shelter and place of sanctuary for weary travelers.

The first mosque ("place of prostration," from the Arabic term *masjid*) was the home of Muhammad in Medina. His dwelling included a large, open courtyard and a covered area to shelter worshipers. The *muezzin*, or caller, climbed to the roof of Muhammad's home to call the faithful to worship. Later mosques were based upon this first place of worship.

During the earliest days of the empire, some of the first mosques were former Christian churches. During the Umayyad period, the construction of new mosques began. These first mosques were designed by architects and built by craftsmen from around the empire: Arabs, Persians, Syrians, and Egyptians all contributed to the design and construction of early mosques. As a result, designers incorporated some of the stylistic elements from their region into the mosque's structure and design. In areas that were once part of the Byzantine Empire, for example, Turkish architects used domes and half domes when designing their mosques. In

Mosque Facts

- The largest mosque built during the Islamic Empire was the Great Mosque at Samarra, begun by the Abbasid caliph Mutasim. The mosque covered 45,500 square yards. Inside, it was paved with marble and supported by marble columns, with enamel tiles covering the walls. The minaret, which is the only feature of the mosque that survives today, was 175 feet tall.
- The Dome of the Rock is one of the oldest Islamic structures in the world. Built in 691, less than six decades after the death of Muhammad, it remains one of the most breathtaking and beautiful sites in Jerusalem.
- One of the largest mosques in the world today is the Hassan II Mosque in Casablanca, Morocco. There is room for about 25,000 worshipers inside the mosque, while 80,000 more can gather outside. Its minaret, the tallest in the world, stretches more than 680 feet into the sky. Construction on the mosque begain in 1986 and it was finished in 1993.

Persia, the former Sassanian Empire, the walls were covered with colored ceramic tiles decorated with Persian patterns.

Throughout the empire, however, the mosques shared a number of basic characteristics. Most were rectangular, with an open courtyard and a covered prayer hall. During the Umayyad period, a minaret, or tower, became standard for newly constructed mosques. Minarets may have been inspired by the lighthouse of Alexandria in Egypt. The muezzin made his call to prayer from the minaret.

Another important mosque feature, the mihrab, was added around the beginning of the eighth century. The mihrab, or prayer niche, enables every Muslim throughout the empire to locate the quibla, the direction of Mecca, where the faithful face when they pray. The mihrab is usually beautifully decorated, with much attention paid to its design. Other mosque characteristics included a fountain for cleansing. In many cases, the mosque's fountain also served as the main well for the town.

The imam, or religious leader, stood on the minbar, a sort of pulpit, to lead the faithful in prayer. The side of the mosque closest to Mecca was the site of the sanctuary, the meeting place for the community. There is no law that requires Muslims to worship in a mosque. However, the mosque enables worshipers to unite as a community of people.

In mosques throughout the Islamic Empire (and in most mosques today), there are separate sections provided where women can worship, apart from men. In the early days of the empire, most women prayed at home. Later, they stood at the back of the mosque and left before the men. Finally, special sections were set aside for them to pray.

Some of the most notable examples of early Umayyad mosques that are still around today are the Dome of the Rock and the Aqsa Mosque in Jerusalem, as well as the Great Mosque in Damascus. These early structures helped give the Umayyads credibility as the successors of Muhammad and the leaders of the Umma. The mosques were all built to outshine Christian churches that stood nearby. The caliph Walid, who commissioned the Great Mosque in Damascus, did not want Muslims to be distracted by churches and Walid's mosque was built over the site of a Christian church. The church's towers were converted into minarets.

These early mosques were made of stone, but included such features as mosaic tiles, decorative patterns, and, in the case of the Dome of the Rock, a beautiful golden dome. As more mosques were constructed throughout the empire, they became even more beautiful and elaborate.

CONNECTIONS >>>>>>>>>>>>>>>>>>>>>>>>>>>>>>>>>>

Arabesque

One type of design that was popular in the Islamic Empire was a swirling, interlocking, pattern of spirals inspired by the way plant leaves and stalks intertwine. This type of pattern became popularly known as arabesque. The forms used within the design varied, but the trademark of an arabesque was the repetition of the pattern. Arabesques were first painted on mosques, but were later used to decorate chests, rugs, tombs, and the walls of private homes. These kinds of abstract, repeated patterns are still popular today on rugs, wallpaper borders, buildings, and many other items.

A decorative arabesque from the Alhambra.

Although Islam forbids statues or portraits of religious figures, other designs were used to decorate the mosques. These included geometric patterns, floral and plant patterns (a Byzantine influence), and animals such as birds, antelopes, lions, dogs, and mythological griffins and dragons (from Persian tradition).

One of the most beautiful mosques in the Islamic Empire was the Great Mosque of Cordoba, built in 785 by amir Abd al-Rahman I, the Umayyad prince who had escaped the Abbasid slaughter of his family. Abd al-Rahman called his mosque the Kaaba of the West. Muslims and Christians alike considered it one of the wonders of the medieval world.

Built on the site where a Christian church and, before that, a Roman temple had stood, the mosque was modeled on Umayyad mosques in Syria and Palestine. Marble taken from nearby Roman ruins supplied the material for 500 columns within the mosque. The columns gave visitors the sensation of being in a forest of stone. Another striking feature of the mosque was its two-tiered, horseshoe-shaped red and white archways. Other unique decorative elements included the mosaic on the mihrab and a main dome decorated with gold mosaic cubes.

The Great Mosque of Cordoba was expanded over about two centuries. At one point, it was the third largest mosque in the Islamic Empire. After the Christian Spanish kings took control of Cordoba in 1236, a cathedral was built in the heart of the mosque. Today, the mosque's minaret is part of the cathedral's bell tower.

Second only to mosques were the royal palaces. The first caliphs to build royal palaces were the Umayyads, who erected big, strong complexes on the edges of the desert near Syria and Jordan. Early palaces included central courtyards, walls, towers, and a gate. Arcades around the open courtyard contained a throne room, a reception room, and living areas for the caliph and his family and courtiers. Early royal complexes often included a large bathhouse, decorated with mosaic tiled floors.

When the Abbasids took power, they had to outdo their predecessors. In Baghdad and other cities throughout the empire, the caliphs built huge palaces made of brick. These palaces became even larger and more ornate as the Abbasids lost control of true political power. Without an empire to run, the Abbasid caliphs turned their attention to spending the wealth of the kingdom by building opulent palaces and other buildings. In Samarra, for example, the Jawsaq Palace, begun in 836, covered more than 430 acres. It included reception rooms, living quarters, harem quarters for the women, pools, gardens, and fountains in the courtyard.

One of the most luxurious royal residences ever built in the empire was the Abbasid palace in Baghdad. The design of the palace was strongly influenced by Persian culture. Visitors approached the wonderful marble structure through a golden gate. The palace was surrounded by gardens with fountains, sculpted figures, blooming trees, and a variety of plants. There was also a zoo on the grounds, home to the many wild, exotic animals collected by the Abbasids. The palace's crowning achievement was the 120-foot-tall green dome, topped by a statue of a horseman bearing a lance.

CONNECTIONS >>>>>>>>>>>>>>>>>>>>>>>>>>>>>>>

Lateen Sails

The lateen sail—a triangular sail that is attached to a short mast—was developed by Arab sailors long before the rise of the Islamic Empire, the lateen sail worked better in cross winds and constantly changing winds than did the square sails favored by other societies. The triangular sails were also easier to handle and could be adjusted and turned in many directions. This made it easier for the ship's crew to change course in narrow waterways.

Later, the Portuguese combined the lateen and square sails to create the caravel, which was used by most explorers during the 15th century, including Bartholomew Diaz, Vasco da Gama, and Christopher Columbus. Along with other navigational innovations, the lateen sail made long-distance sea voyages possible by enabling ships to sail against the prevailing winds. Today, small sailboats around the world can still be seen flying lateen sails, especially in the Mediterranean Sea.

Arab sailors in an illuminated manuscript from 1222–1223.

Inside, goods from all over the empire decorated each room. Tapestries and brocades stitched with gold thread hung from the walls. Mosaic tiles, colored glass, carved wood, and stucco carvings were everywhere one looked. For a special occasion, one Abbasid caliph created the Hall of the Tree to house a huge artificial tree of gold and silver. On the branches, automated silver and gold birds sang tunes for astounded guests.

Storehouse of Knowledge

During the Abbasid Dynasty, the Islamic Empire became known as the light of the world. Here, knowledge and learning were nurtured and encouraged. Arabic translations of Greek works, along with Islamic advances in learning, laid the foundations for modern science, medicine, and other fields of learning.

Many Greek works were translated during the reign of Caliph Mamun (r. 813–833). Some of these works were seized when Muslims conquered Byzantine and Sassanian areas. In other cases, the caliphs sent out groups of scholars to find Greek writings in other cities, including Constantinople.

To facilitate translation and learning, Mamun founded the House of Wisdom in Baghdad. The House of Wisdom included a library, a translation bureau, and a school. There was also an observatory from which scholars and scientists could study the stars and planets—and even discover new ones. At its height, the House of Wisdom had as many as 90 scholars working on translations. From Spain and Sicily, these translations eventually made their way into the Western world, where they were translated into Latin.

Philosophy and History

The ninth century saw the emergence of many important Islamic philosophers. Islamic philosophy, like other areas of knowledge, was profoundly influenced by the Greek masters. Islamic philosophers most frequently focused on themes that touched on religion, especially the relationship of logic and reasoning to the Quran and Sunna.

One of the most famous philosophers of the empire was Abu al-Walid Muhammad ibn Rushd (1126–1198), known in the West as Averroës. Known as the Great Commentator, Ibn Rushd was born in Cordoba, Spain, while it was under Muslim control. As a young man, he studied the works of the ancient Greeks, including Aristotle and Plato. He later served as the caliph's physician and a judge.

One of Ibn Rushd's most famous works of philosophy was *On the Harmony of Religion and Philosophy*, written in 1190. The book includes chapters on "The Creation of the Universe," "Divine Justice and Injustice," and "The Day of Judgment." However, his thoughts on the soul and other religious matters covered in the book put him in hot water with Muslim authorities. He was declared a heretic and banished from Cordoba in 1195.

Ibn Rushd's works were eventually translated into Latin, the language of European scholars at the time. They provided the foundation for a famous theological work begun in 1265 by Catholic scholar Thomas Aquinas. Aquinas's work, *Summa Theologica*, is considered one of the greatest philosophical treatises to come out of Europe during the Middle Ages.

The most famous Islamic historian was Al Biruni (973-1048). In addition to writing one of the first Arab histories, Biruni was also a noted geographer and scientist. His *Chronology*, written in 1030, offered an account of the histories of ancient empires of the world that included information on their festivals, calendars, and rituals. His most famous work, however, was *Kitab al-Hind*, a book that described the history and geography of India.

Medicine

Among the most important Islamic contributions were their advances in the field of medicine. By applying and adding to Greek medical theory, the physicians of the empire were the most advanced of their time. European Crusaders (see page 49) who came into contact with Islamic medicine brought home some of these treatments, which helped advance European medical practices of the day.

Most early Islamic physicians were Persian. The Persians had embraced the Greek medical theory of Galen and Hippocrates before the Muslim conquest. One of the most talented and learned Persian physicians was al-Razi (c. 865–925). Known as "the Experienced," Razi wrote more than 100 medical

CONNECTIONS >>>>>>>>>>>>

Influential Doctor

The Persian physician al-Razi made long-lasting contributions to general science as well as medicine. His classification of all things into three major groups—animal, vegetable, and mineral—is still used today. He also described and used beakers, flasks, vials, and crystallization dishes during experiments. These items are still used in chemistry labs today.

Monumental Medical Advances

Islamic contributions to medicine were monumental. Many of the practices that Muslim physicians described, improved, or pioneered are still used today in one form or another. Advances in medicine during the empire included:

The pharmacy. In *A History of the Arab Peoples*, Albert Hourani writes, "It has been said that the pharmacy as an institution is an Islamic invention." Because of the vast Islamic trading network, Muslim physicians had access to many new drugs. Muslim scholars wrote volumes dedicated to the properties and effects of various simple and compound drugs. They also were the first to create a systematic method of determining dosages for medicines. Pharmacology was considered an important profession. Beginning in the early 800s, pharmacists, like doctors, had to pass examinations and become licensed.

Surgical milestones. At a time when European clergymen were encouraging doctors to stop performing any type of surgery, Muslim physicians were forging ahead in successful efforts to cure their patients surgically. They performed operations to remove bladder stones, cataracts and other eye diseases, and varicose veins. They also created many new surgical instruments and pioneered the use of anesthesia, especially opium, to render a patient unconscious before surgery. The anesthesia was administered by holding a drug-soaked sponge underneath the patient's nose.

Understanding disease. The Muslims were among the first to understand that many diseases are contagious. In the 14th century, Ibn al-Khatib described how disease is spread (quoted in Bernard Lewis's *A Middle East Mosaic*): "The existence of contagion is established by experience, study, and the evidence of the senses, by trustworthy reports on transmission by garments, vessels, ear-rings; by the spread of it by persons from one house, by infection of a healthy sea-port by an arrival from an infected land." Muslim doctors were the first to describe the differences between smallpox and measles, and to identify scabies and anthrax.

Hygiene and health. Some of the most important contributions to medical knowledge by Islamic physicians came in the field of hygiene and its relationship to health. They were the first to describe the germ-killing effects of alcohol and to use the substance in hospital settings. The idea of a healthy environment was also pioneered by the Muslims: To determine the healthiest setting for a new hospital in Baghdad, the famous physician al-Razi hung slabs of meat in various parts of the city. The area where the meat rotted most slowly was chosen as the hospital's new site.

Record keeping. Islamic hospitals were probably among the first to keep medical records on all patients. The records included information on the patient's condition and treatment.

CONNECTIONS >>>>>>>>>>>>>>

Scientific Words with Arabic Origins

alchemy: from *al-kimiya*, meaning the sciences of alchemy and chemistry

alcohol: from *al-kuhl*, meaning ground cosmetic powder, later used to describe refined or distilled substances

algebra: from *al-jabr*, the joining together of disorganized parts

borax: from *buraq*, a white, powdery mineral used in cleaning and soldering

camphor: from *kafur*, a strong-smelling tree gum often used in medical ointments

elixir: from *al-iksir*, in medieval alchemy, a material that would change other metals to gold; later, the term became synonymous with a cure-all

nadir: from *nazir*, the lowest point; the opposite of zenith

pancreas: from bancras

zenith: from *samt*, the highest point

zero: from *sifr*, which was translated into Latin as *zephyrum*, and then into Italian as *zero*

books. He was the first person to document the symptoms of smallpox, thus differentiating it from other similar diseases. This documentation made diagnosis and treatment of the disease more effective. Razi also wrote about immobilizing broken bones using a plaster substance.

Razi was especially interested in the relationship between hygiene and sickness. Many centuries before germs and bacteria were identified, the Islamic physician believed that sick people should be kept in a clean environment. His most famous and sought-after work was a huge, private notebook of medical essays that included Greek, Persian, Syrian,

Hindu, and Arabic information. Called *Kitab al-Hawi fi al-tibb* (comprehensive book on medicine), the book influenced medical practices throughout Europe.

People throughout the empire took the practice of medicine quite seriously. Not just anyone could become a physician. Men had to have special training and pass tests on anatomy and the writings of Galen. Specialists had to have even more knowledge of the field they were practicing in. Beginning in 931, some caliphs required doctors to be licensed.

Islamic doctors used a number of methods to treat sick patients, including acupuncture, drugs, and ointments. Some treatments seem remarkably similar to ones used today. For example, a physician might recommend that a patient with a stomach ailment follow a special diet. Someone with a serious wound might be prescribed a healing poultice or ointment.

However, some treatments were quite unusual by today's standards. In addition to bloodletting, doctors might try cupping–placing hot glasses on the skin's surface to draw the blood upward. Cupping, which was also practiced in Asia, was thought to be good for curing headaches and purifying the blood.

Doctors made medicines out of a wide variety of materials. They used balsam, ginger, and various fruits, plants, and herbs to create healing potions. Some drugs were made with animal and metal products. Although most physicians mixed up their own medicines and ointments, there were also pharmacies, where mixing and storing drugs was overseen by an inspector.

Islamic physicians performed various types of surgeries, usually based on ancient Greek methods. Surgeons used drainage tubes, anesthetics (including opium), and cauterization–techniques that are still used today. They amputated diseased arms and legs and operated on cataracts of the eyes. In fact, ophthalmology, the medical study of the eye, was one area in which Islamic physicians excelled. The first book on ophthalmology and the eye's structure and functions was written by Hunayn ibn Ishaq, a Persian who studied medicine in Baghdad during the middle of the ninth century. Islamic doctor Abu Ali al-Hasan ibn al-Haytham (965–c.1040), known as Alhazen in the West, is remembered today as the father of optics. He discovered that vision is the result of rays of light reflecting off objects and passing into the eye.

The first Islamic hospital was built in Baghdad in the early ninth century. Before long, there were more than 30 hospitals throughout the

Contributions to Astronomy

As in other areas of science, Islamic intellectuals excelled in astronomy. Islamic scientist al-Battani (c. 858–929) more precisely calculated the length of a solar year than anyone had ever done before. He calculated 365 days, 5 hours, 46 minutes, 24 seconds; the most recent measurement is 365 days, 5 hours, 48 minutes, and 45.5 seconds. The Polish astronomer Copernicus (1473–1543), who proposed the theory that all planets in the solar system rotate around the sun, mentioned his debt to al-Battani in one of his books.

Islamic scientists were the first to make use of the observatory as a scientific institution. From observatories in Baghdad, Cairo, and other places in the empire, Abul Wafa (940–998) and other astronomers watched and described the movements of the sun, planets, and stars. In the 16th century, Danish scientist Tycho Brahe (1546–1601) watched the movements of the moon and made the same "discoveries" Islamic astronomers had made centuries earlier. From an observatory in Egypt, al-Battani catalogued close to 500 stars.

As the empire was being torn apart in the early 1250s, Islamic scholars continued to make advances in the field of astronomy. In 1274, Muslim astronomer Nasir al-Din al-Tusi (1201–1274) convinced the Mongol invaders to allow him to build a huge observatory in what is today northwest Iran. The observatory at Maraghah was a center for astronomical research for many years and would provide a model for future observatories.

empire. In remote areas, traveling clinics set up tents and sick villagers were treated and medicated, if necessary.

At Islamic hospitals, any sick person, regardless of their culture or religion, would be treated. In the larger hospitals, patients were separated into wards depending upon their illness. There was also a special ward for the mentally ill. Islamic hospitals also had something similar to the modern-day emergency room. Here, minor illnesses that did not require hospitalization were treated.

The most famous physician of the Islamic Empire was Abu-Ali al-Husayn ibn Sina (980–1037), known in the West as Avicenna. Ibn Sina, born near Bukhara (in what is today Uzbekistan), began practicing medicine when he was just 18 years old. He later served as the personal physician to the Sultan of Bukhara. Over the years, Ibn Sina also became interested in philosophy, physics, mathematics, astronomy, and even musical theory.

Milestones in Ibn Sina's career include his descriptions of skin diseases and psychological illnesses. He was the first person to realize that tuberculosis is infectious, and that some diseases are spread by water and soil. For cancer, his treatment is still timely today: Treat the illness during its earliest stages and remove all the diseased tissue. Ibn Sina's best-known work was *Al-Qanafi'l Tibb* (the canon of medicine). This encyclopedia of medical knowledge was studied throughout the Islamic empire and in European universities from the 12th through the 17th centuries.

Astronomy and Geography

Astronomy, the study of the stars and the planets, was an important field of study in the Islamic Empire. A useful science, astronomy helped people find their way on land or at sea. Astronomy was also approved by the Quran, which states, "[Allah] has appointed for you the stars that by them you might be guided in the shadows of land and sea."

Even before Islam, Arabs had been interested in the sky. Early Arabs named certain planets and stars, using these heavenly bodies to guide them safely across the desert. After the conquest began, Islamic scholars used information garnered from the ancient peoples of Persia, Greece, and India to improve and advance the field of astronomy.

One way in which astronomy affected the Islamic Empire was through the Islamic calendar. Unlike the solar-based Gregorian calendar used by most Western countries today, the Islamic calendar is based on the cycles of the moon. Like the Gregorian calendar, the Islamic calendar has 12 months.

Brains and Beauty
This brass astrolabe was made by Muhammad Zaman al-Mashadi in Iran in the 17th century. It is used to measure the angles of planets and stars.

Making Sense of Math

Mathematics was just one area in which Muslim scholars clearly excelled. Many of the mathematical theories developed during the height of the Islamic Empire made possible the advancement of arithmetic, geometry, algebra, and other branches of mathematics. Perhaps most importantly, Muslim scholars made mathematics useful and practical.

The Muslims owed much of their early knowledge of mathematics to texts written by ancient Greeks and Hindus. Islamic scholars then expanded upon the Greek and Hindu information, developing and advancing concepts and theories. Centuries later, texts written in the Islamic Empire would inspire and teach European scholars.

One of the most significant Islamic contributions to math was popularizing a new system of numerals borrowed from the Hindus. These numerals, which are now known as Arabic numerals, are the same symbols that are used today to denote numbers. Before this time, numbers were represented with letters of the alphabet or with Roman numerals, which were difficult to work with.

The new numeral system enabled merchants and others to more quickly and efficiently solve math problems without the use of an abacus (a counting device using beads strung on wires) or a process known as "finger reckoning." Finger reckoning, or counting on the fingers, was widely used by merchants be-fore the introduction of Arabic numerals. By using the new numbers, problems could now be solved with pen and paper.

A second important Muslim contribution to mathematics also originated with the Hindus: a system of arithmetic based on 10 and including zero. Before the use of zero, those solving math problems had to arrange their numbers in columns to differentiate one from another. The use of the base-10 system and zero made arithmetic logical and practical, and was adopted by European mathematicians centuries later. The zero also enabled Muslim scholars to further develop the decimal system and fractions.

Muslims also advanced other Hindu concepts, taking square and cube roots to fourth, fifth, and even higher roots.

Another branch of mathematics that blossomed during the Islamic Empire was algebra. Algebra (which comes from the Arabic term *al-jabr*, or "the joining together of disorganized parts"), was more fully developed by Muslim mathematicians. They pioneered the use of linear, quadratic, and cubic equations. They also devised a step-by-step process to solve problems, called an algorithm. The concept of "x" as the unknown variable in algebraic equations came about from a Spanish translation of the Arabic word *shay*, or "thing." Geometry and trigonometry were also advanced by Muslim scholars.

These months alternate between 29 and 30 days each. There are also periodic leap years. Because it is a lunar calendar, though, the Islamic calendar falls about 11 days behind the solar calendar each year. As a result, the calendar fails to follow the seasons.

The calendar was created in 638 by the order of caliph Umar. Umar wanted the calendar to begin in the year one with the Hijra, Muhammad's migration to Medina and the birth of Islam. Therefore, in the Islamic calendar every date after July 16, 622, is marked A.H., or after the Hijra.

The Islamic empire was much more advanced in its knowledge of geography than were other regions of the world at that time. While Islamic scientists embraced the Greek theory that the Earth was round, for example, most people in Europe still believed that it was flat.

The need to advance in this field of learning was driven by the size of the empire. Travelers from one area to another needed accurate maps and guidebooks to help them get where they needed to go. As a result, guidebooks with the names of roads, towns, and distances from one place to another became quite common. Guidebooks of other lands were written as well, including China, India, and Russia.

Islamic mapmakers worked together with astronomers to produce a view of the sky and the Earth that was more accurate and comprehensive than ever before. As a result, maps from the Islamic Empire were highly valued by ship's captains throughout the world. Islamic explorers also had a number of other advantages. For example, Islamic sailors used lateen sails—triangular sails that made their ships faster than ships using square sails.

The astrolabe was an ancient Greek invention used to pinpoint the position of stars. It was widely used by Islamic scholars. Called "the mathematical jewel," the astrolabe consisted of a flat metal disk with degrees marked around the outer edge. A pivot and pointer were attached at the instrument's center. By pointing the astrolabe at the stars, scientists were able to determine their positions, as well as the movement of the planets. Islamic scientists also calculated the circumference and diameter of the Earth more accurately than ever before; they came within 4 percent of the Earth's actual circumference.

Mathematics, Chemistry, and Physics

Mathematics was a field of knowledge that had many applications in the ancient Islamic world. It assisted scholars studying astronomy, and had the more practical uses of aiding in trade, commerce, and surveying.

Some of our most basic mathematical concepts, including Arabic numerals, the idea of zero, and the decimal system, were spread to the West through the Islamic Empire. These concepts, however, were borrowed from other cultures. For example, Arabic numerals, which we use for numbers today, were taken from the Hindus. These concepts enabled people to work with large numbers without having to use words or letters.

CONNECTIONS >>>>>>>>>>>>>>>>

The Scientific Method

In their quest to turn base metals into gold, scientists of the Islamic Empire made a number of advances that contributed greatly to the development of modern science, particularly chemistry and physics. These scientists translated and studied the works of ancient Greek, Persian, and Indian scholars, then developed and enhanced them. But scientists throughout the empire—Muslims, Christians, and Jews—also made many original contributions to the sciences.

Islamic scientists perfected what is known today as the scientific method. This method includes carefully conducting, documenting, and duplicating experiments. The scientific method is used by scientists around the world and is taught to students in science classes.

One of the outstanding minds of the Islamic Empire was a man named Jabir ibn Hayyan, known to the West as Geber (c. 721–815). Jabir (and later, those writing under his name) improved methods of crystallization, distillation, calcination, reduction, and evaporation. He also prepared a number of new chemical substances. His books are among the oldest known works on chemistry, and Jabir is sometimes called the "father of chemistry."

Another important Islamic scientist and philosopher was al-Kindi (c. 801–873), who wrote more than 200 works on physics and other matters. Topics that interested al-Kindi included optics, the reflection of light, weights, meteorology, and tides. Nearly four centuries after his death, al-Kindi's book on optics, *De Somniorum Visione*, served as a resource for Roger Bacon and other scientists.

Islamic scholars enjoyed puzzling over difficult mathematical concepts and equations. They even created puzzles for one another to solve. Some of these puzzles are still worked on by mathematicians today. The love of advanced mathematical concepts led to advancements in algebra, geometry, and trigonometry, all areas that had been originally developed by the ancient Greeks. The Islamic scholar al-Khwarizmi (c. 780–850) wrote an algebra text book that was used in Europe until the 16th century.

Islamic scholars also made major contributions to the field of chemistry, although unwittingly. Throughout the empire, men worked to turn base metals such as iron into gold through a combination of magic and science. This study was known as alchemy, and it was the medieval predecessor of chemistry. Through alchemy, scholars gained a better understanding of compounds and how they are formed. They also developed information on refining metals, dyeing cloth, distilling vinegar, and manufacturing glass.

Epilogue

DESPITE THE MONGOL CONQUEST OF THE ISLAMIC EMPIRE, the power of Islam remained strong. Eventually the Mongol conquerors became Muslims themselves, and within 50 years they had named Islam as their state religion. Although the empire itself was dead, Islam was still alive and stronger than ever. In the coming centuries it continued to expand, spreading to all corners of the world.

One of the last great Islamic states was the Ottoman Empire, which eventually controlled Turkey, the Balkans, and Asia Minor. The Ottomans claimed the title of caliph in the 16th century, redefining the term and requirements of office to accommodate the fact that they were not members of the Quraysh. The Ottoman Empire lasted until 1922. After that time, many nations that had once been part of the Islamic Empire fell under European control, becoming colonies of countries such as Great Britain and France. During the struggles to gain self-government, the idea of taking up arms in a jihad against the West again gained strength among many Muslims.

The 20th century witnessed a revitalization of Islam. Following World War II, most of the colonies of the European powers gained their independence. These included all the Middle Eastern states, which were predominantly Islamic (except Israel).

Although some states, such as Turkey, turned away from certain Islamic traditions, other nations embraced the religion. Some nations returned to the idea of Islam as both a religion and a guiding political force. In the middle of the century, a number of states sprang up that include Islamic laws in their legal codes, including Pakistan (1947), Indonesia (1949), Sudan (1956), and Malaysia (1963).

OPPOSITE
Friday Prayers
Worshipers at a mosque in Kemang, Indonesia. Islam is a far-flung religion, and today, the majority of Muslims are not Arabs.

The 20th century also marked the birth of two Muslim theocratic governments in Iran (1979) and Afghanistan (1996). In these two nations, the chief Islamic religious leader was also the recognized head of government. As in the time of the Islamic Empire, government and law were based on sharia. With the break-up of the former Soviet Union in 1991, Central Asian states with large Muslim minorities also emerged onto the world scene. Such nations include Kazakhstan and Uzbekistan.

Islam continues to be a strong political force around the globe and a unifying factor, drawing people from many nations together with a common bond of a shared religion. In 1969, the Organization of the Islamic Conference (OIC) was founded by 30 Islamic states to represent Muslim nations around the world. Today, 56 nations are part of the OIC. The group's stated mission is to "speak with one voice to safeguard the interest and ensure the progress and well-being of their peoples and other Muslims in the world over."

Jihad Today

Today, many Americans think of bloodshed and violence when they hear the word jihad. Jihad, however, means more than just holy war. It also means a constant struggle or striving on behalf of God. In the earliest days of Islam, it meant the struggle to live the way God commanded, to resist sin and wrongdoing, and to act justly. It also included sacrificing one's life—if necessary—in that struggle, as a *shahid*, or martyr.

Later, jihad came to mean the wars of conquest to spread the word of Muhammad. Jihad also requires Muslims to wage war when the Umma is threatened by invasion, foreign rule, or forced conversion. Then they are defending their faith.

While some Muslims do interpret jihad in a broader, bloodier sense, most do not. Examples of extremist groups who have appropriated the term jihad include the Jamaat al-Islamiyya in Palestine, the Muslim Brotherhood in Egypt, and al-Qaeda, an international terrorist group led by Osama bin Laden (b. 1957). These three groups, as well as several others, have caused death and destruction around the world. Most Muslims believe these extremist views misrepresent true Islamic teachings and values.

The Challenge of Fundamentalism

In recent years, a number of radical fundamentalist Muslim groups have taken up terrorism to advance their own agendas. Such groups as al-Qaeda, led by Osama bin Laden, have identified the United States, Saudi Arabia, and other nations as corrupting influences on Islam, and have made them targets of terrible violence.

One of the most deadly attacks took place on September 11, 2001. Terrorists from the al-Qaeda network hijacked planes and flew them into the World Trade Center in New York and the Pentagon building in Washington, D.C. Another plane crashed in Pennsylvania. During the suicide attacks, more than 3,000 people were killed.

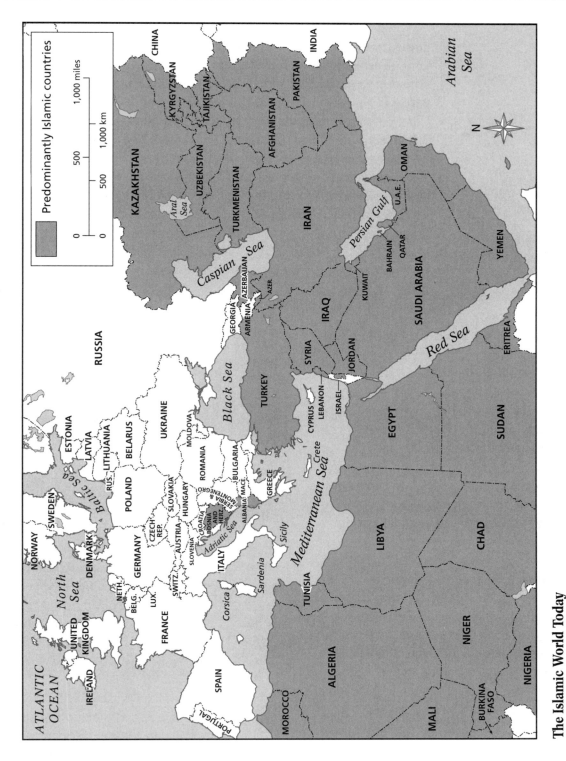

The Islamic World Today
The influence of the Islamic Empire is clear in this map, which shows how many nations continued to embrace Islam even after the empire crumbled.

After the attacks, many Muslims around the world spoke out against these terrorist actions. Despite the strong condemnation by most Muslims, some Americans vilified Islam as a whole. A number of American Muslims were attacked verbally and physically, and mosques became the target of vandalism and graffiti.

Many conflicts between Muslims and other groups in the Middle East have centered on the issue of Israel and its refusal to set aside land for an independent Palestinian state. Numerous terrorist attacks and suicide bombings have wracked Israel over the years, met with equally violent reprisals by the Israeli armed forces. In 2002, Israel averaged five terrorist attacks each month. In 2003, talks between Israeli and

CONNECTIONS >>>>>>>>>>>>>>>>>>>>>>>>>>>>>>>>

Iran: A Modern Theocracy

There are very few modern theocracies. One is the Islamic Republic of Iran. Since 1979, Iran's government has been headed by a Muslim religious and political leader called the faqih. The faqih is appointed by an Assembly of Experts and holds his job for life. He is the ultimate expert in interpreting Islamic law and how it applies to Iran's government. The faqih has the power to accept or veto any laws passed by the rest of the government. He also controls the country's armed forces and judiciary system.

Iran also has an elected president and several appointed cabinet ministers. The president is the second most important person in Iran, after the faqih. According to Iran's constitution, the president must be a Shiite Muslim. He has the power to appoint ministers, sign laws, and veto any actions taken by the cabinet ministers.

All civil and criminal law in Iran is based on Shiite Islamic law. Chief justices, judges, and attorney generals must be religious men.

Iranians vote for their president and representatives. This photo was taken during the 2004 elections.

CONNECTIONS >>>>>>>>>>>>>>>>>>>>>>>>>>>>>>>>

English Words, Arabic Roots

Every day, every time we speak, the lasting impact of the Islamic Empire can be heard in the hundreds of words that have Arabic roots. These words include the following.

ENGLISH	ARABIC	ENGLISH	ARABIC
admiral	*amir al* (commander of)	magazine	*makhazin* (storehouse)
alcove	*al-qubba* (arch)	massage	*massa* (to stroke)
almanac	*al-manakh*	mattress	*matrah* (place where something is thrown)
apricot	*al-birquq*		
artichoke	*al-kharshuf*	safari	*safari* (journey)
candy	*qandi* (crystallized sugar)	sequin	*sikka* (place where coins are minted)
coffee	*qahwa*		
cotton	*qutun*	sofa	*suffa* (carpet, divan)
ghoul	*ghul*	syrup	*sharab*
giraffe	*zirafa*	tabby	from *al-Attabiya*, a district in Baghdad where striped cloth was made
guitar	*qitar*		
jar	*jarra* (earthen water vessel)		

Palestinian leaders continued. Palestinians hope for an independent state, while Israelis need to be assured of their future safety.

There has also been division within Muslim nations themselves. Moderate, progressive Muslims have encountered heavy opposition from more traditional, conservative groups. Conservative Muslims worry that Western influences will weaken and erase the traditions that have persisted in Islamic countries for centuries. Women who speak out for equality are jailed in some countries, as are students who try to introduce Western ideas of free speech and democracy.

Despite the struggles within Islam, the religion remains a strong and vital one throughout the world. Islam continues to attract new followers every day, and remains one of the fastest growing religions in the world. According to Adherents.com, a web site featuring statistics on the world's major religions, there are an estimated, 1.3 billion Muslims in the world today. That is nearly 20 percent of the world population (based on the U.S. Census Bureau's online World Population Clock). Only Christianity has more adherents.

TIME LINE

570	Muhammad is born in Mecca.
632	Muhammad dies in Medina. Abu Bakr becomes the first caliph of the Islamic Empire.
633–640	The Muslims conquer Syria and Iraq.
639–641	The Muslims attack and eventually take control of Egypt.
642–654	The Muslims conquer Persia.
650	An official version of the Quran is assembled.
661	Muawiya becomes caliph, founding the Umayyad Dynasty. Damascus becomes the capital. Muslims split into Sunnis and Shiites; the Shiites do not recognize Umayyad authority.
680	Husayn (son of Ali) is killed at Karbala.
691	The Dome of the Rock is built by Caliph Abd al-Malik.
696	Arabic becomes the official language of the empire.
705–720	The Muslims conquer Central Asia, India, and Spain.
747–750	The Abbasid revolution overthrows Marwan II and establishes the Abbasid Dynasty.
756	Abd al-Rahman establishes the Umayyad emirate of Cordoba.
762	The city of Baghdad is founded.
830	Caliph al-Mamun establishes the Bayt al-Hikma (House of Wisdom) to translate classical texts into Arabic.
909	The Fatimid caliphate takes control of North Africa and, in 969, Egypt. Cairo becomes its capital.
945	The Buyids take control of Baghdad, leaving the Abbasid caliphs as figureheads.
1096	The First Crusade is launched by Europeans to take control of the Holy Lands (today's Israel) from the Muslims.
1187	Saladin re-conquers Jerusalem from the Crusaders.
1236–1266	Muslims lose all of Spain except Granada.
1258	Mongol invaders from the east take over Persia and eventually take control of Baghdad, bringing an end to the Islamic Empire.
1492	Granada, the last Muslim stronghold in Spain, is defeated by the army of Catholic monarchs Ferdinand and Isabella. Muslims are given the option to convert or leave.

RESOURCES: Books, Video

Books

Editors of Time-Life Books. *What Life Was Like in the Lands of the Prophet* (New York: Time-Life Inc., 1999)
> A colorful look at the Islamic world from 570 to 1405. Beautiful illustrations, maps, and interesting sidebars are included.

George, Linda S. *The Golden Age of Islam* (Salt Lake City, Utah: Benchmark Books, 1998)
> Covers the civilization of the Islamic Empire from the last years of the eighth century to the 13th century.

Hilliam, Paul, and Nick Ford. *Islamic Weapons, Warfare, and Armies: Muslim Military Operations Against the Crusaders* (New York, Rosen Publishing, 2003)
> An in-depth look at the military tactics used by Muslim armies against the Crusades during the Middle Ages.

Newby, Gordon D. *A Concise Encyclopedia of Islam* (Oxford, England: Oneworld Publications, 2002)
> Everything you ever wanted to know about the people, places, and practices of Islam. Includes alphabetical listings.

Ries, Julien. *The World of Islam* (Broomall, Penn.: Chelsea House Publishers, 1999)
> The beginnings and basic beliefs of Islam are covered in this book. Fascinating full-color graphics.

Robinson, Francis, editor. *The Cambridge Illustrated History of the Islamic World* (New York: Cambridge University Press, 1999)
> Facts about Islam's history and practice are presented, along with its economic, social, and intellectual structures. There are excellent graphics and maps, and boxes throughout provide more depth on key issues.

Video

Grupper, Jonathan. *Islam: Empire of Faith* (Alexandria, Va.: Gardner Films and PBS Home Video, 2000)
> Re-enacted and actual scenes make the beginnings of the Islamic Empire come to life on this film, available in both DVD and VHS formats.

RESOURCES: Web Sites

Encyclopaedia of the Orient
www.lexicorient.com/e.o/
> An encyclopedia of geographical, historical and current information on the nations of the Middle East and North Africa. You can search by place name, person, or country.

Islam: Empire of Faith
www.pbs.org/empires/islam
> A companion site to the public television program (and video) of the same name, the site contains information about the faith, culture, and innovations of the Islamic Empire, and profiles of important figures.

Islamic Arts and Architecture Organization
www.islamicart.com/index.html
> This site, sponsored by the Islamic Arts and Architecture Organization, covers all facets of Islamic art and architecture, including calligraphy, rugs, and mosques. It also includes a history of the Islamic Empire, greeting cards, downloads, a museum directory and interesting links to other sites.

Islamic Culture and the Medical Arts
www.nlm.nih.gov/exhibition/islamic_medical/islamic_00.html
> This site from the National Library of Medicine takes you on a tour of a virtual museum exhibit chronicling the many important contributions Islamic doctors have made to medicine. Includes original drawings and pages form ancient medical texts.

Islamic History Sourcebook
www.fordham.edu/halsall/islam/islams-book.html
> This site contains a wealth of information and primary source material from the pre-Islamic world through today. It includes maps and Islamic music that can be played as you browse the site.

The Islamic World to 1600
www.ucalgary.ca/applied_history/tutor/islam/
> This series of lessons from the University of Calgary is a multimedia introduction to the first millennium of Islamic history. It outlines Muslim beliefs and practices, as well as the history of the Islamic world from the 7th to the 17th centuries, including the expansion of the Islamic empires of Asia, Africa, and Europe. External and internal links, maps and plenty of images make this a really comprehensive, very interesting site.

Muslim Heritage
www.muslimheritage.com
> This site presents a wide overview of the contributions of Muslim scientists, writers and artists. It includes an excellent interactive timeline of Islamic history.

BIBLIOGRAPHY

Adherents.com, "The Largest Muslim Communities," URL: http://www.adherents.com/largecom/com_islam. html. Updated January 27, 2000.

Ahmed, Akbar S., *From Samarkand to Stornoway: Living Islam*. New York: Facts on File, 1994.

Armstrong, Karen, *Islam: A Short History*. New York: Random House, 2000.

Beverley, James A., *Islamic Faith in America*, New York: Facts on File, 2003.

Cartage, "The Poets of Arabia, Selections." URL: http://www.cartage.org.lb/en/Themes/ GeogHist/ histories/histdocs/Biblio13/A13/Poetry/arabianpoets1. html. Posted 1999.

Council on American-Islamic Relations, "The Mosque in America: A National Portrait." URL: http://www.cair-net.org/mosquereport/Masjid_Study_Project_2000_ Report.pdf. Report published April 26, 2001.

Esposito, John L., Ed., *The Oxford History of Islam*. New York: Oxford University Press, 1999.

Farah, Caesar E., *Islam*. New York: Barron's Educational Series, 2000.

FitzGerald, Edward, translator, *Rubaiyat of Omar Khayyam*. London: Penguin Books, 1985.

Glassé, Cyril, *The Concise Encyclopedia of Islam*. New York: HarperCollins, 1991.

Gordon, Matthew S., *Islam: Origins, Practices, Holy Texts, Sacred Persons, Sacred Places*. New York: Oxford University Press, 2002.

Graduate Center of the City University of New York, "American Religious Identification Survey 2001." URL: http://www.gc.cuny.edu/studies/aris_part_two.htm. Published October 2001.

Grupper, Jonathan. *Islam: Empire of Faith* (DVD). Gardner Films, 2000.

Halsall, Paul, *Medieval Islamic Sourcebook: Pre 622*. "The Hanged Poems," URL: http://www.fordham.edu/ halsall/source/640hangedpoems.html. Published 1998.

Hitti, Philip K., *The Arabs: A Short History*. Washington, D.C.: Regnery Publishing, 1996.

Hourani, Albert, *A History of the Arab Peoples*. Cambridge, Mass.: The Belknap Press of Harvard University Press, 1991.

Jandora, John Walter. *Militarism in Arab Society: An Historiographical and Bibliographical Sourcebook*. Westport, Conn.: Greenwood, 1997.

Lewis, Bernard, *The Arabs in History*. New York: Oxford University Press, 2002.

——, *A Middle East Mosaic: Fragments of Life, Letters, and History*. New York: Random House: 2000.

——, *The Middle East: A Brief History of the Last 2,000 Years*. New York: Scribner, 1995.

——, *The Muslim Discovery of Europe*. New York: W.W. Norton & Co., 2001.

Lewis, Brenda Ralph, Ed., *Great Civilizations*. Bath, U.K.: Parragon Publishing, 1999.

Newby, Gordon D., *A Concise Encyclopedia of Islam*. Oxford, U.K.: Oneworld Publications, 2002.

Racy, A.J., "Arab Music," Turath.org. URL: www.turath. org. Published 2002.

Renard, John, *Responses to 101 Questions on Islam*. New York: Paulist Press, 1998.

——, *Windows on the House of Islam: Muslim Sources on Spirituality and Religious Life*. Berkeley, Calif.: University of California Press, 1998.

Robinson, Francis, Ed., *Islamic World*. New York: Cambridge University Press, 1996.

Savage-Smith, Emilie, "Islamic Culture and the Medical Arts," National Library of Medicine. URL: http://www. nlm.nih.gov/exhibition/islamic_medical/islamic_00.html. Updated April 15, 1998.

Stewart, Desmond, *Early Islam*. New York: Time Inc., 1967.

Suhufi, Sayyid Muhammad, *Lessons from Islam*. Karachi, Pakistan: Prima Printers, 1999.

Swisher, Clarice, Ed., *The Spread of Islam*. San Diego, Calif.: Greenhaven Press, 1999.

Time-Life Books, *What Life Was Like in the Lands of the Prophet*. Alexandria, Va.: Time-Life, 1999.

Watt, W. Montgomery, *Muhammad: Prophet and Statesman*. Oxford University Press, 1961.

Wilson current biographies online, URL: vnweb. hwwilsonweb.com.

INDEX

Page numbers followed by *i* indicate illustrations.